THE COLOR 4 FUN SAMPLER

COLOR 4 FUN

COLORING BOOKS

Introduction

Color 4 Fun LLC was founded in June 2015. It has published more than one dozen coloring books for colorists of all skill levels. Some, like "Romantic Italy," for example, were created in collaboration with uniquely skilled international artists and focus on a singular theme. "Dances of the World" and "A Day at the Circus" are also examples of this approach.

The purpose of this "sampler" is to offer the colorist an introduction to the illustrations of our artists without the need to purchase an entire book containing the work of an unknown artist. Our hope, naturally, is that you will become sufficiently attracted to the illustrations of one or more of the artists in this book and be motivated to buy their book or books.

Happy coloring!

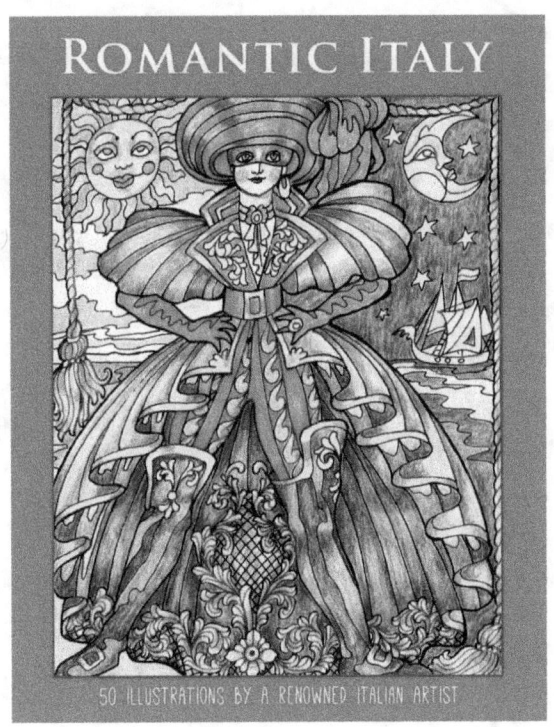

Why do newlyweds from every country in the world choose Italy for their honeymoon? Of course, it is because Italy is recognized as the world's epicenter of love and romance. The beautiful illustrations in this book will virtually transport you to this magical land.

Augusta Schinchirimini's exceptional artistic talent and her passion for the culture of her native land have allowed her to produce 50 illustrations that epitomize Italy's classic art tradition. They are also highly suggestive of the romance that is pervasive in the land of Romeo and Julliet.

Augusta's illustrations will: (a) invite you to join the ostentatious merriment of Carnevale in Venice; (b) reacquaint you with the classic fables of childhood including Pinocchio, Cinderella, Sleeping Beauty and Peter Pan; (c) take you into enchanting gardens filled with flowers, birds and butterflies; (d) escort you through forests filled with animals, castles, and bridges; immerse you among the creatures of the undersea world; and (e) show you classic designs used to make Italy's incomparable "Maiolica" ceramics. "Romantic Italy" is unique among coloring books in that each and every illustration was drawn by hand. Unlike other coloring books, the only "software" used in the creation of this book were the delicate hands of the artist.

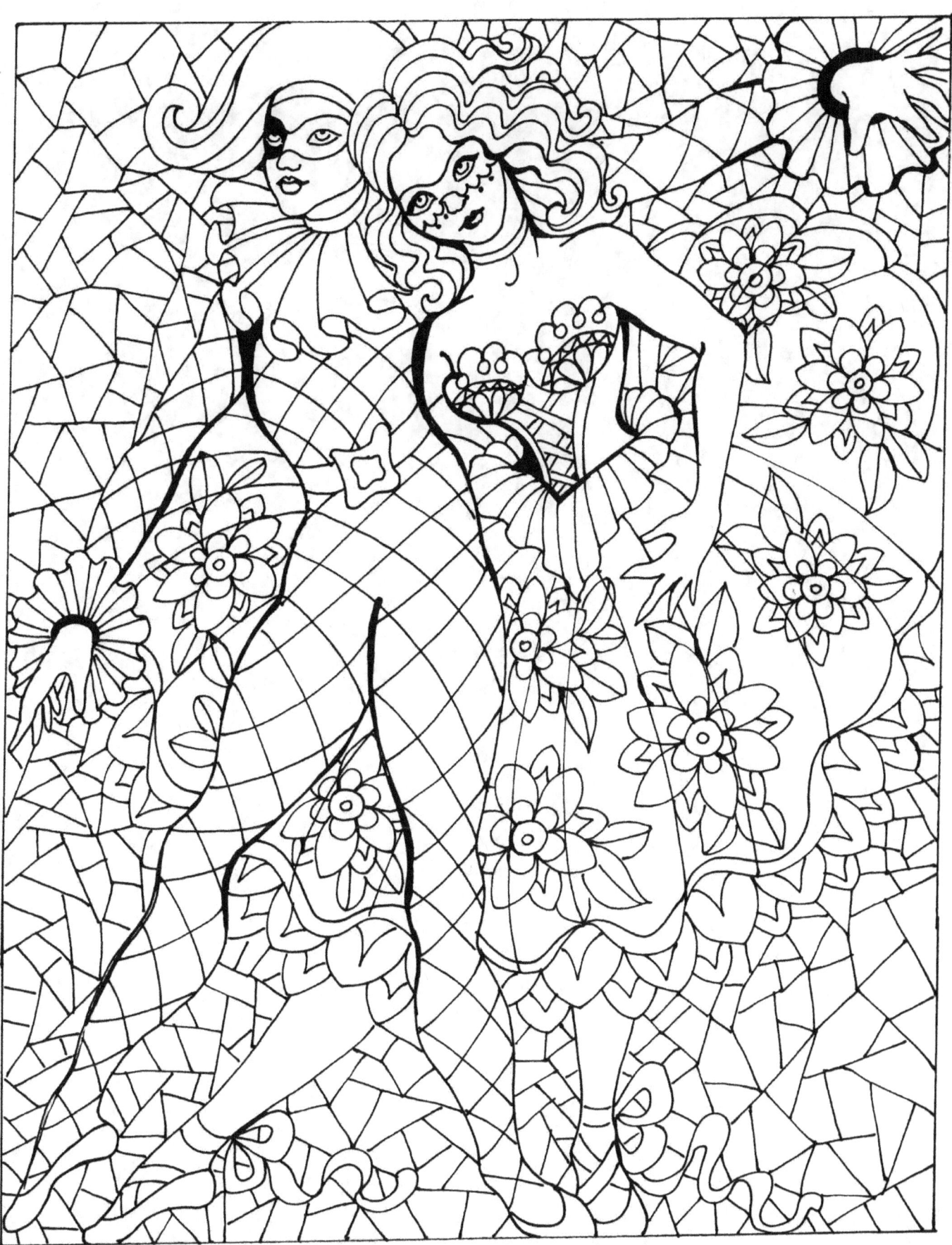

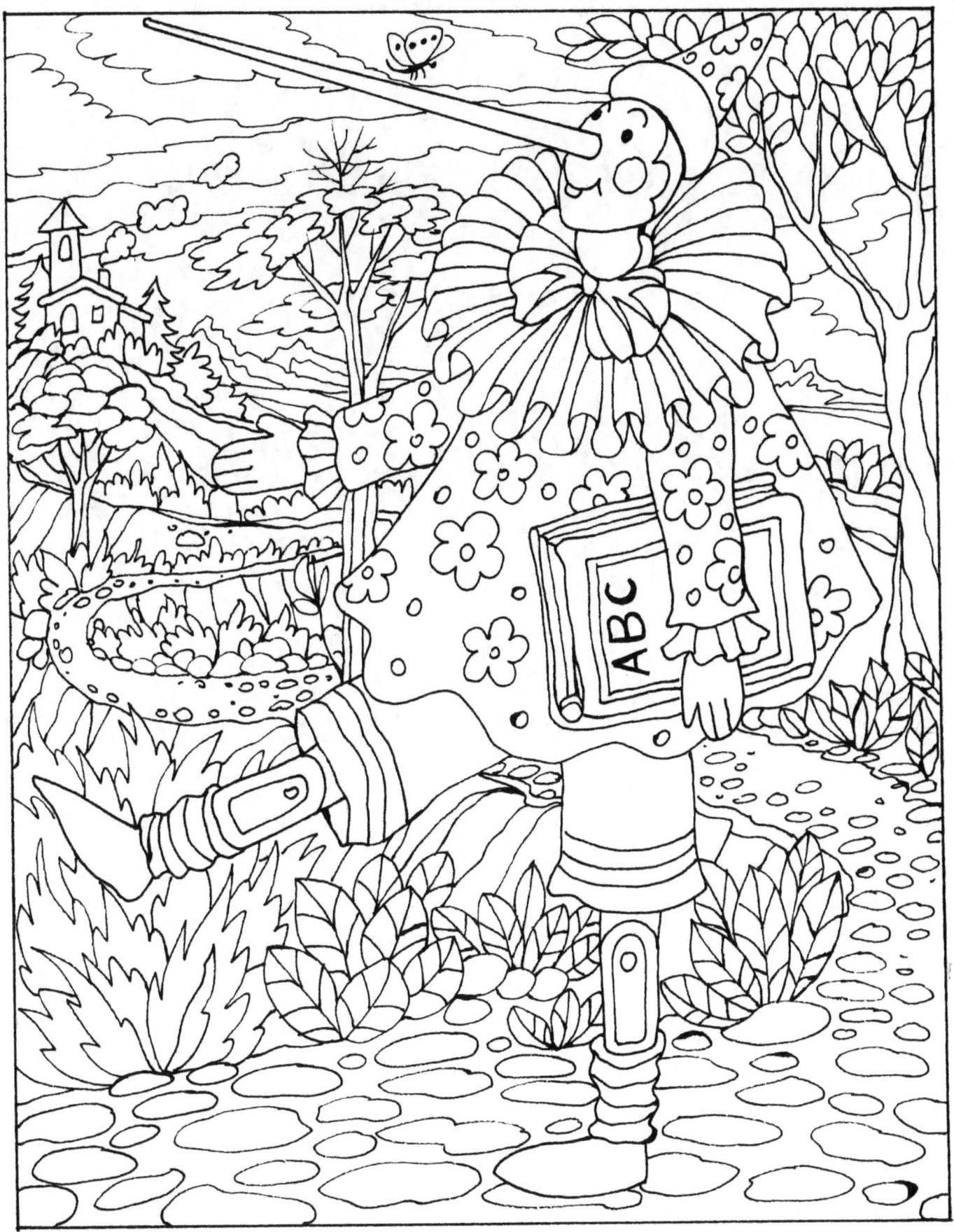

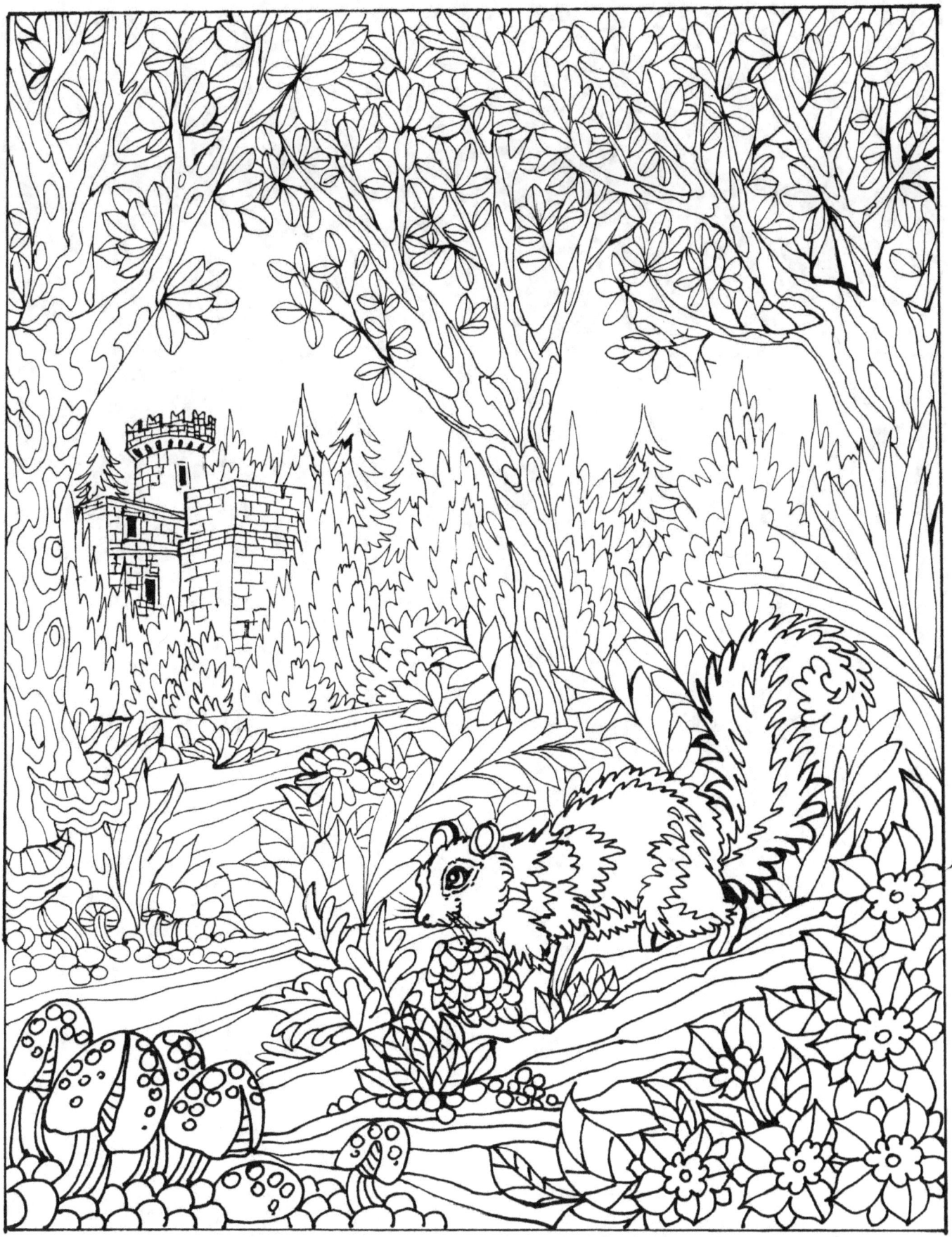

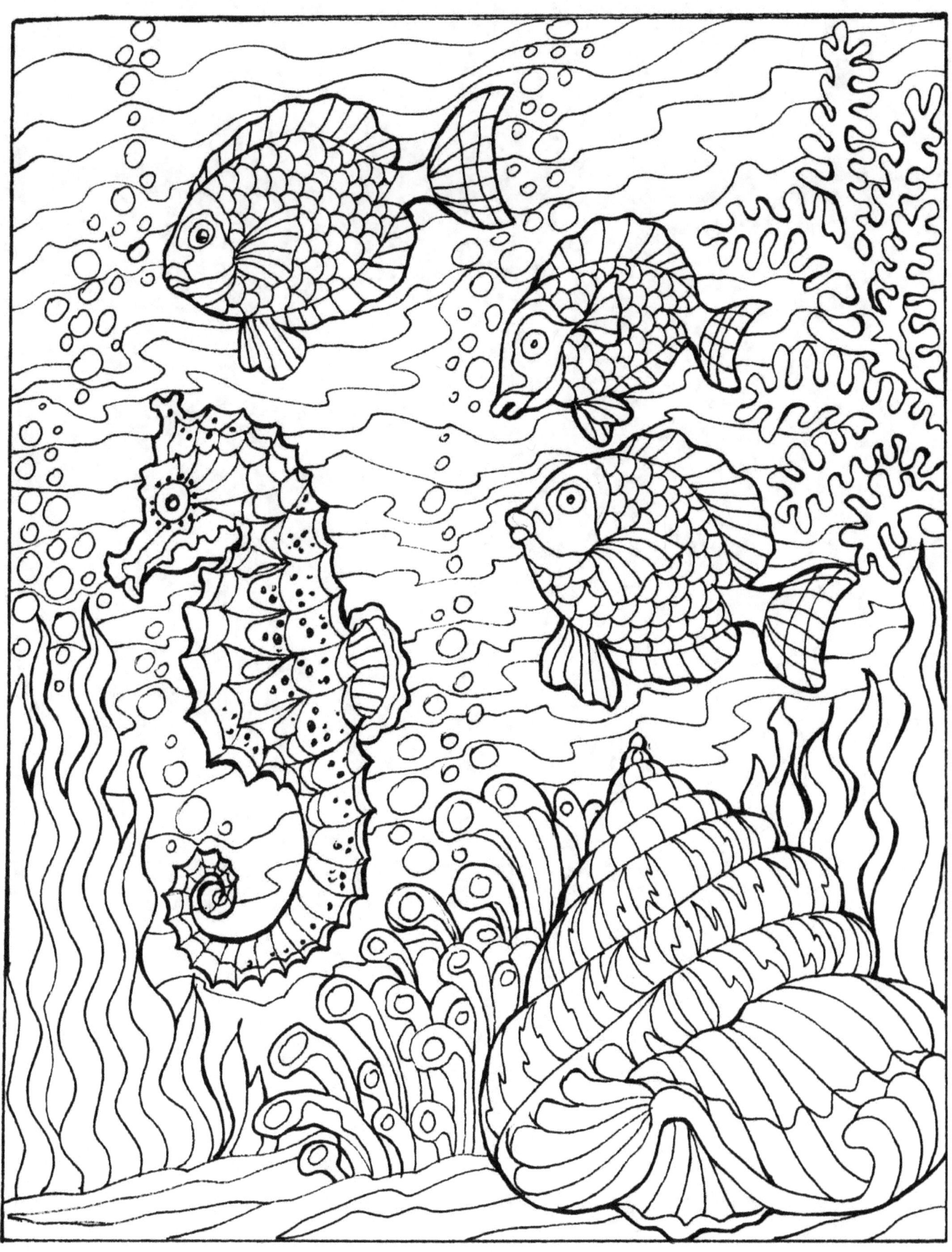

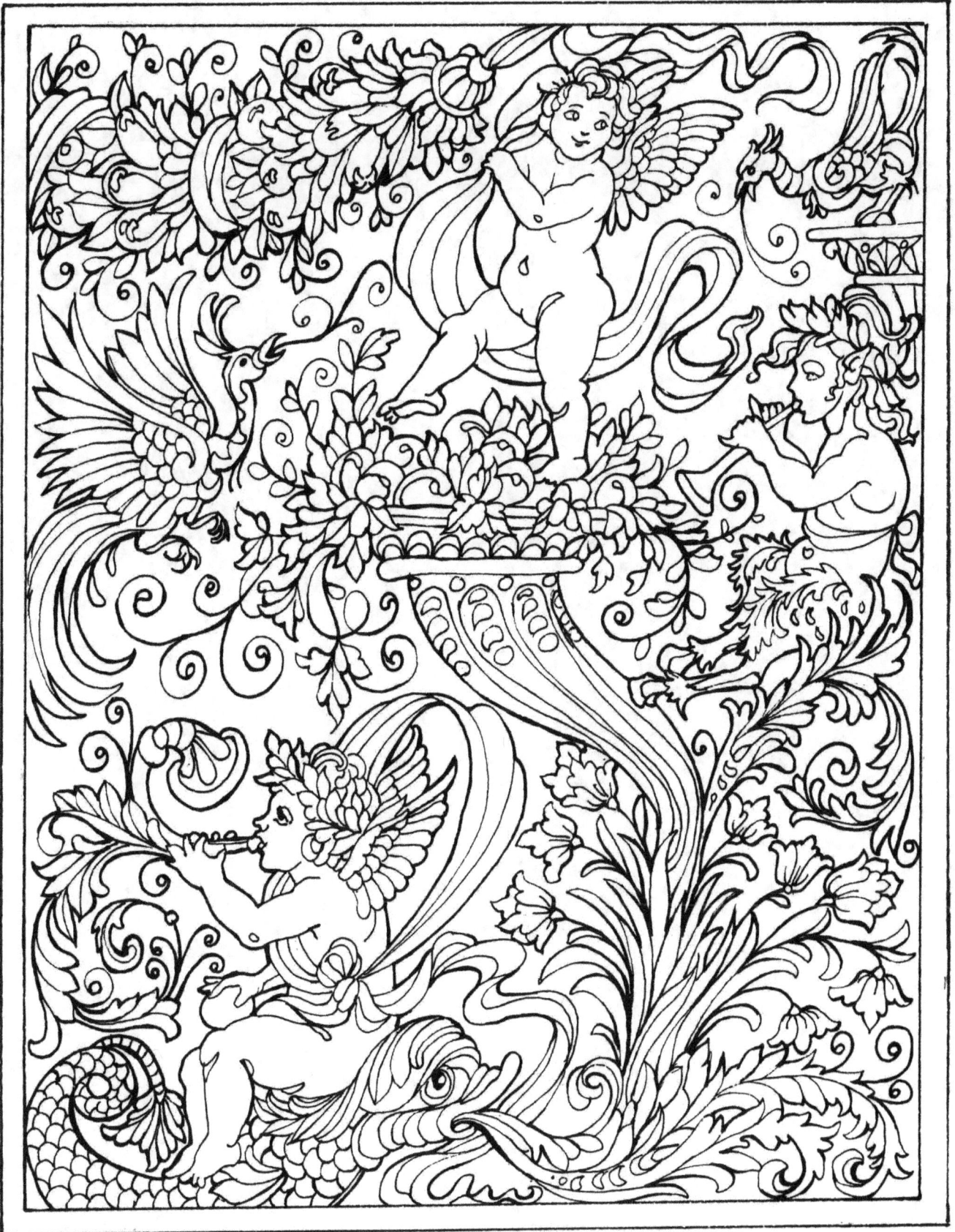

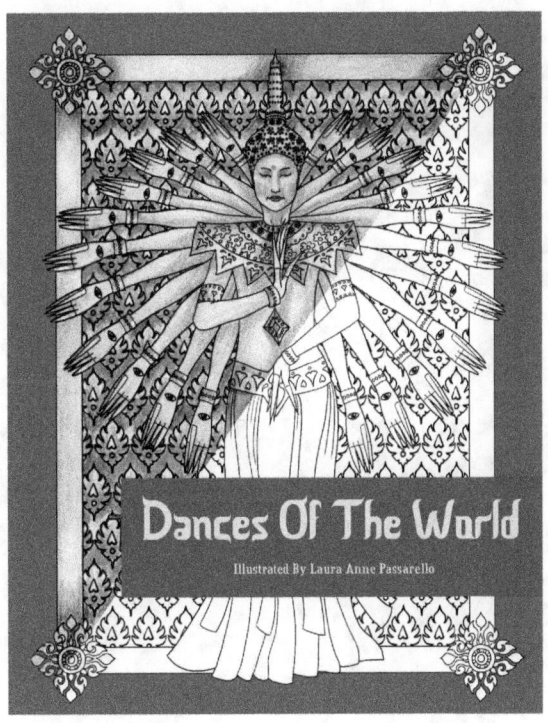

Laura Anne Passarello, the Canadian illustrator of "Dances of the World," has captured the unique aspects of traditional dance across many of the diverse cultures of the world. Dance has been an important form of cultural expression throughout human history.

Laura Anne's 36 illustrations make it possible to take a virtual journey spanning the Americas, the Caribbean Islands, Europe, Asia and the islands of the Pacific Ocean. In addition to well-known dances such as France's can can and Argentina's tango, you'll find exotic dances such as odissi of India and the aspara of Cambodia. And, the dancers' festive costumes represent invitations for the application of abundant color.

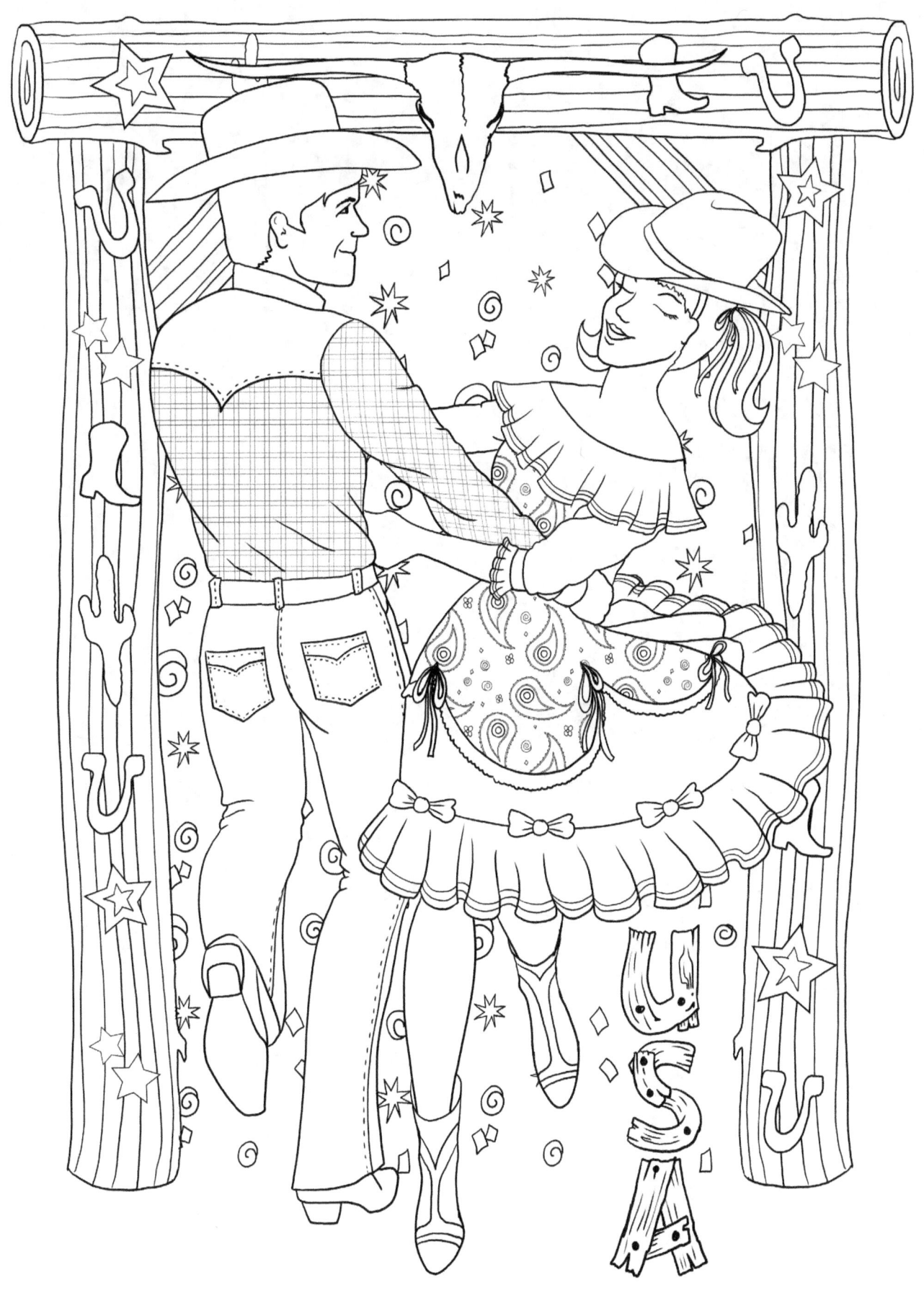

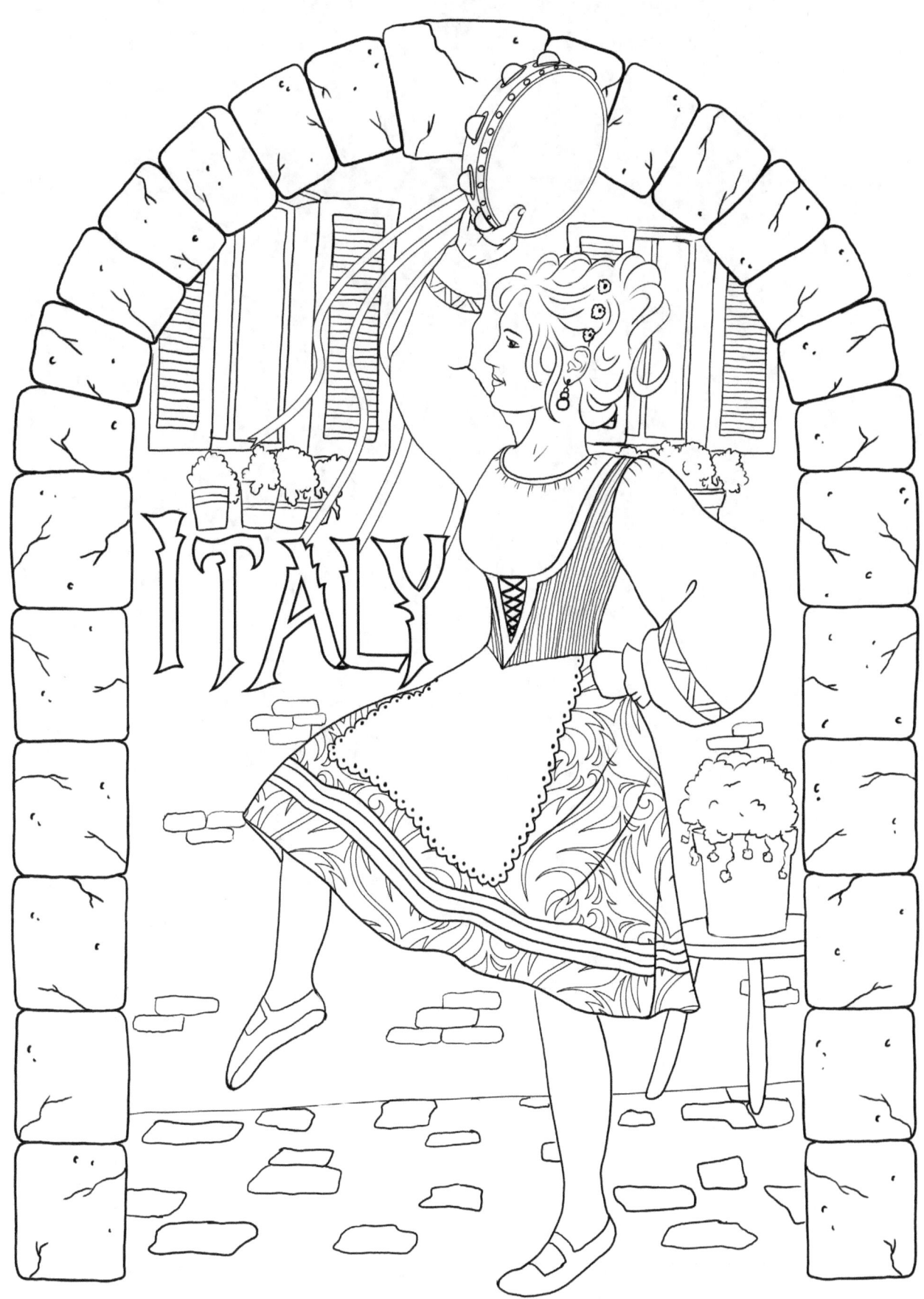

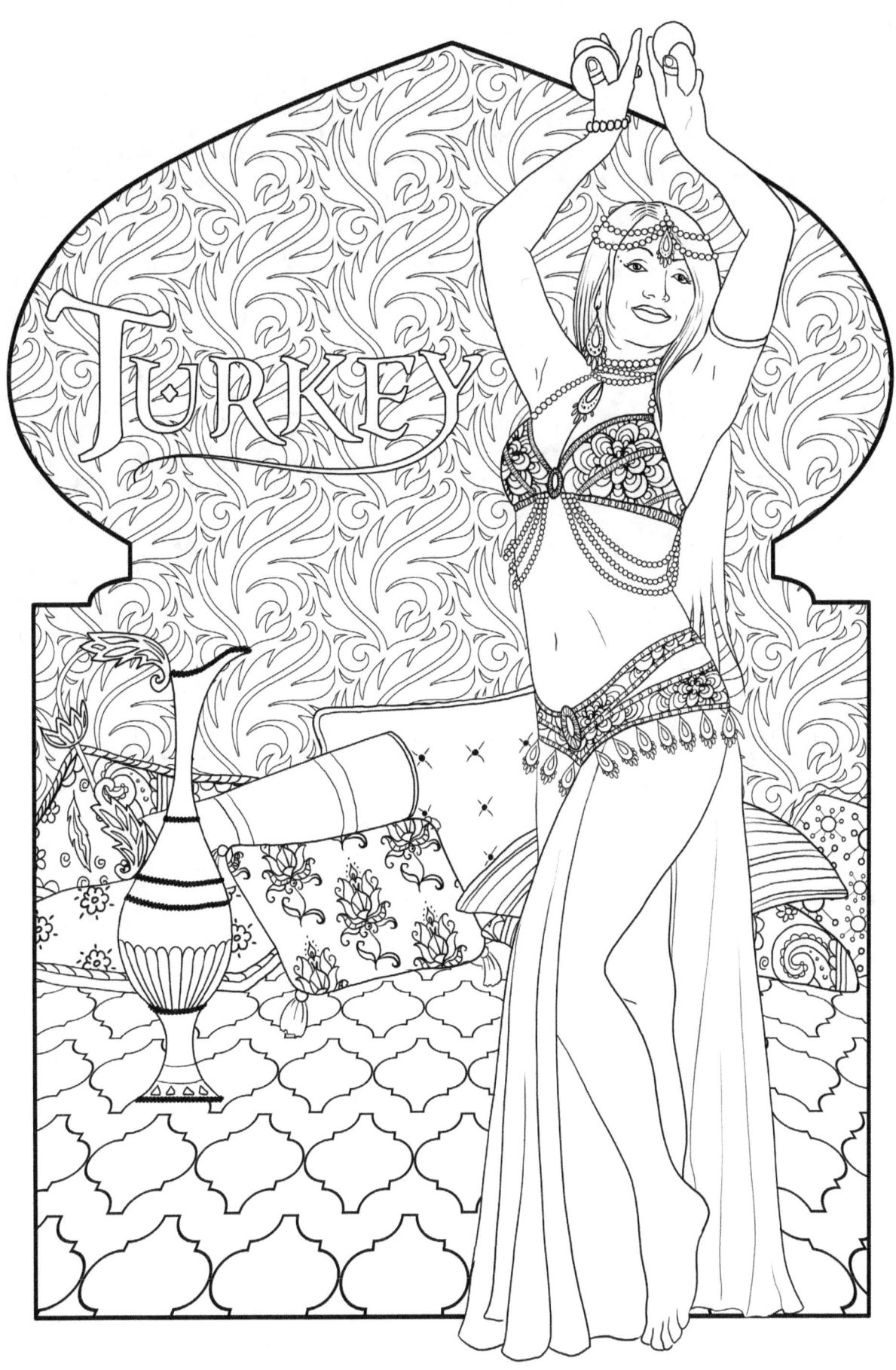

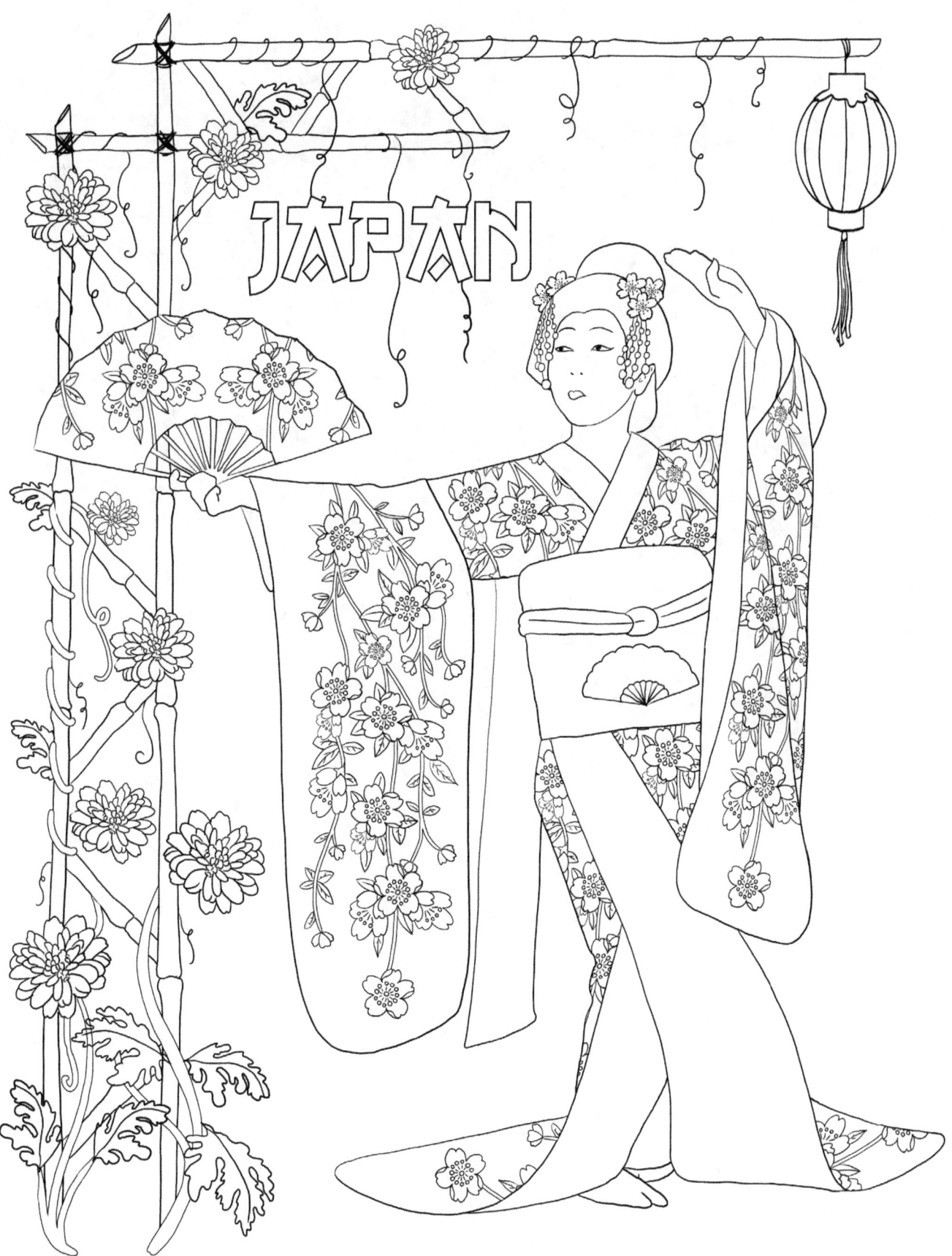

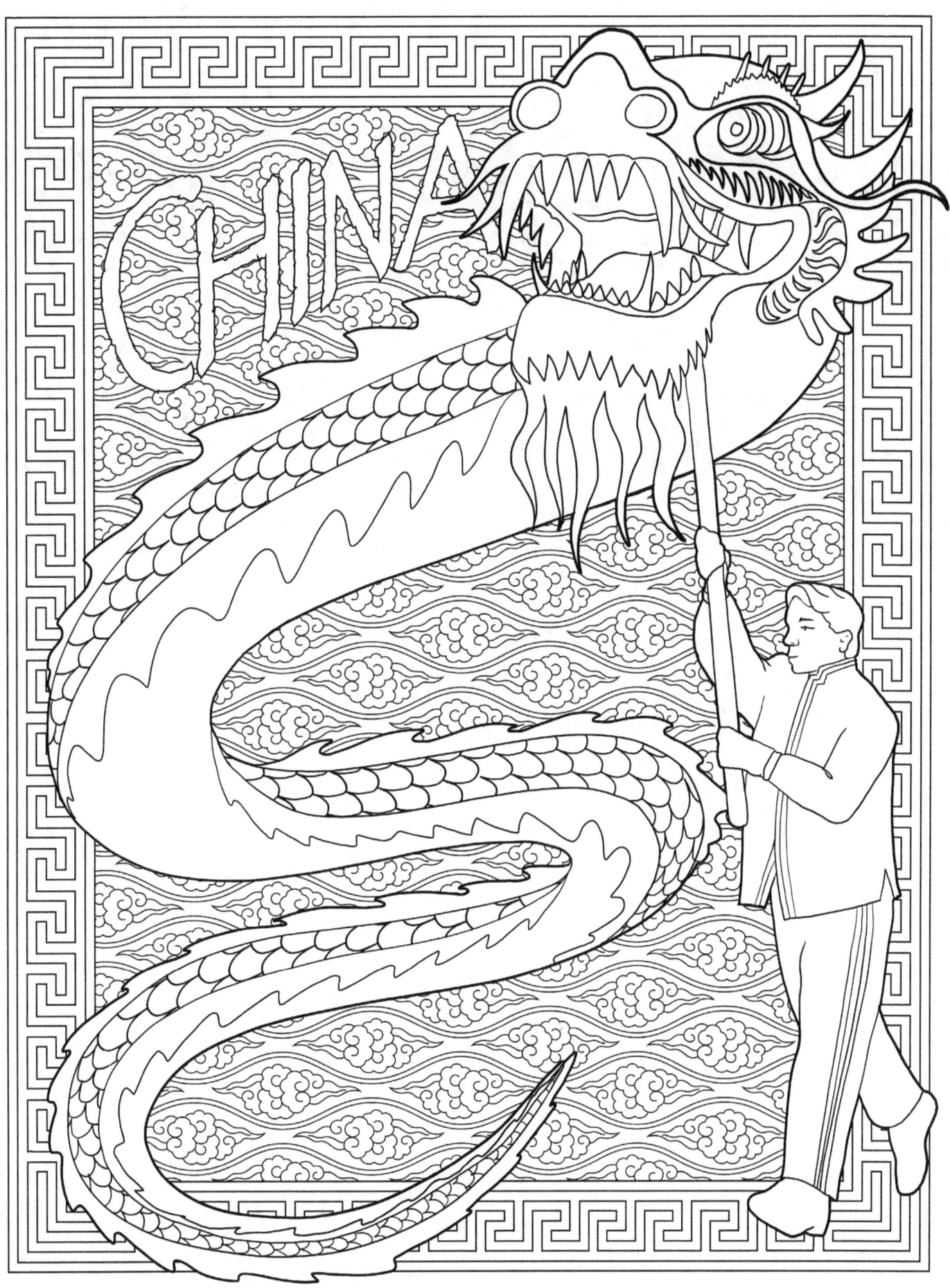

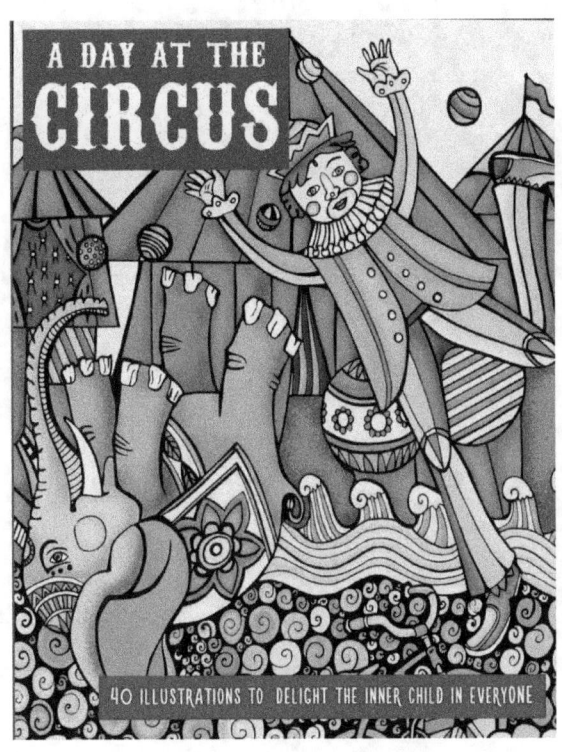

The book's 40 illustrations by Luciana Guerra of Buenos Aires, Argentina, capture the essence of the magical experience provided by attending a circus. She has populated "A Day at the Circus" with clowns, magicians, jugglers, trapeze artists, fortune tellers, strong men, lions, tigers, horses and bears and many of the other performers typically found at the circus.

Luciana's illustrations will most assuredly stimulate your creativity; and they will liberate the inner child residing in each of us as they virtually transport us to the enchanting world of the circus. Go ahead, have some fun!

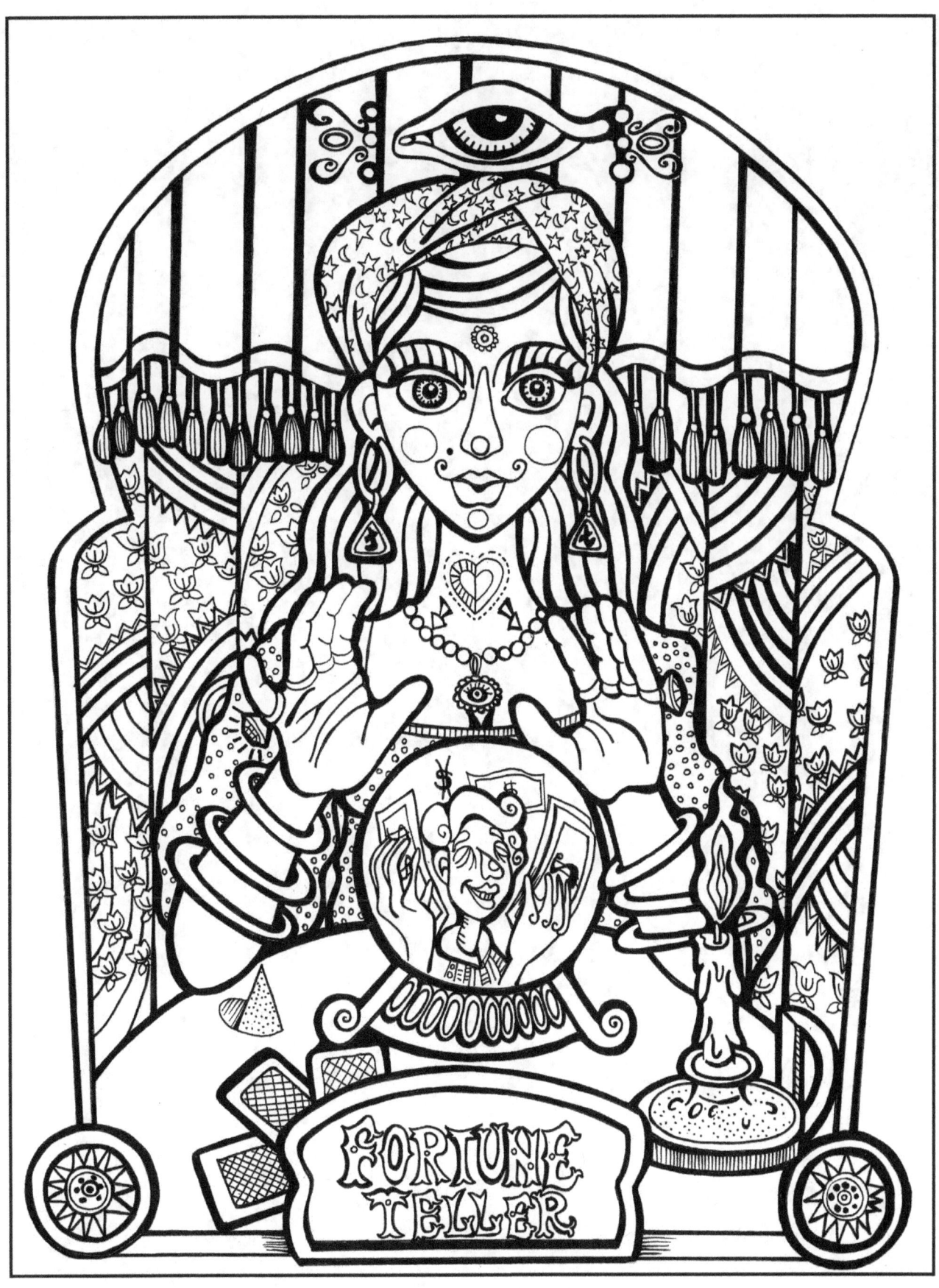

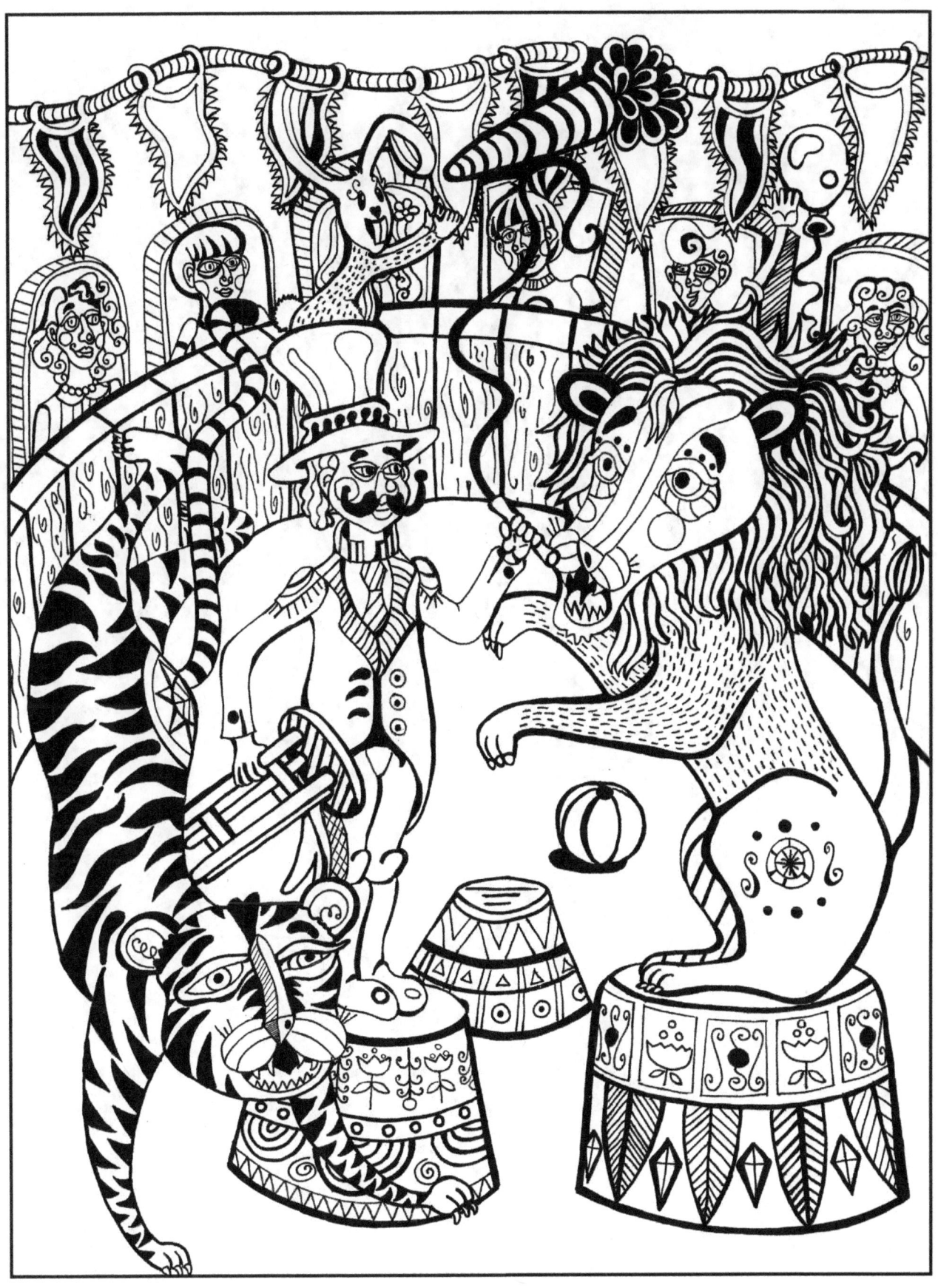

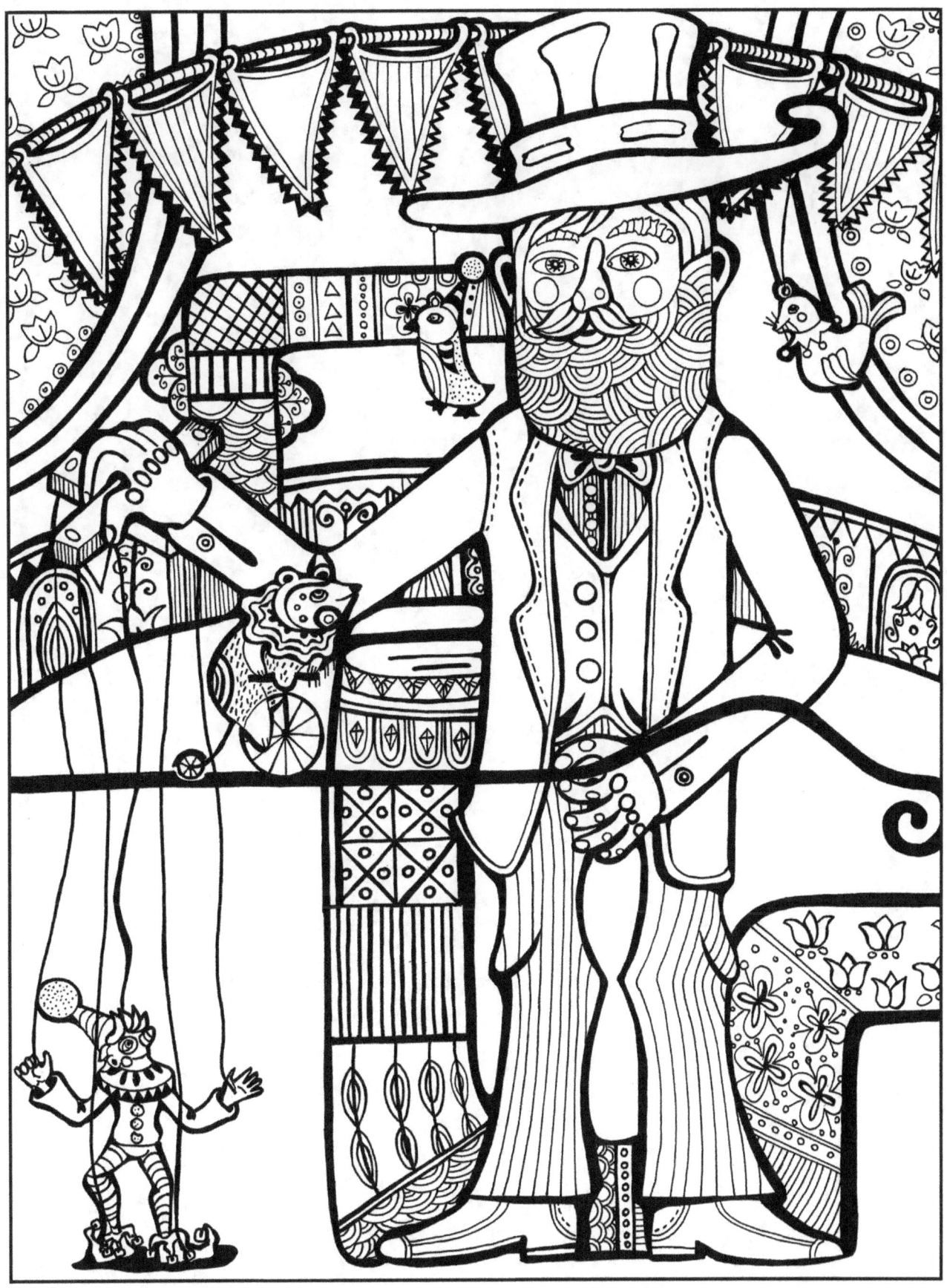

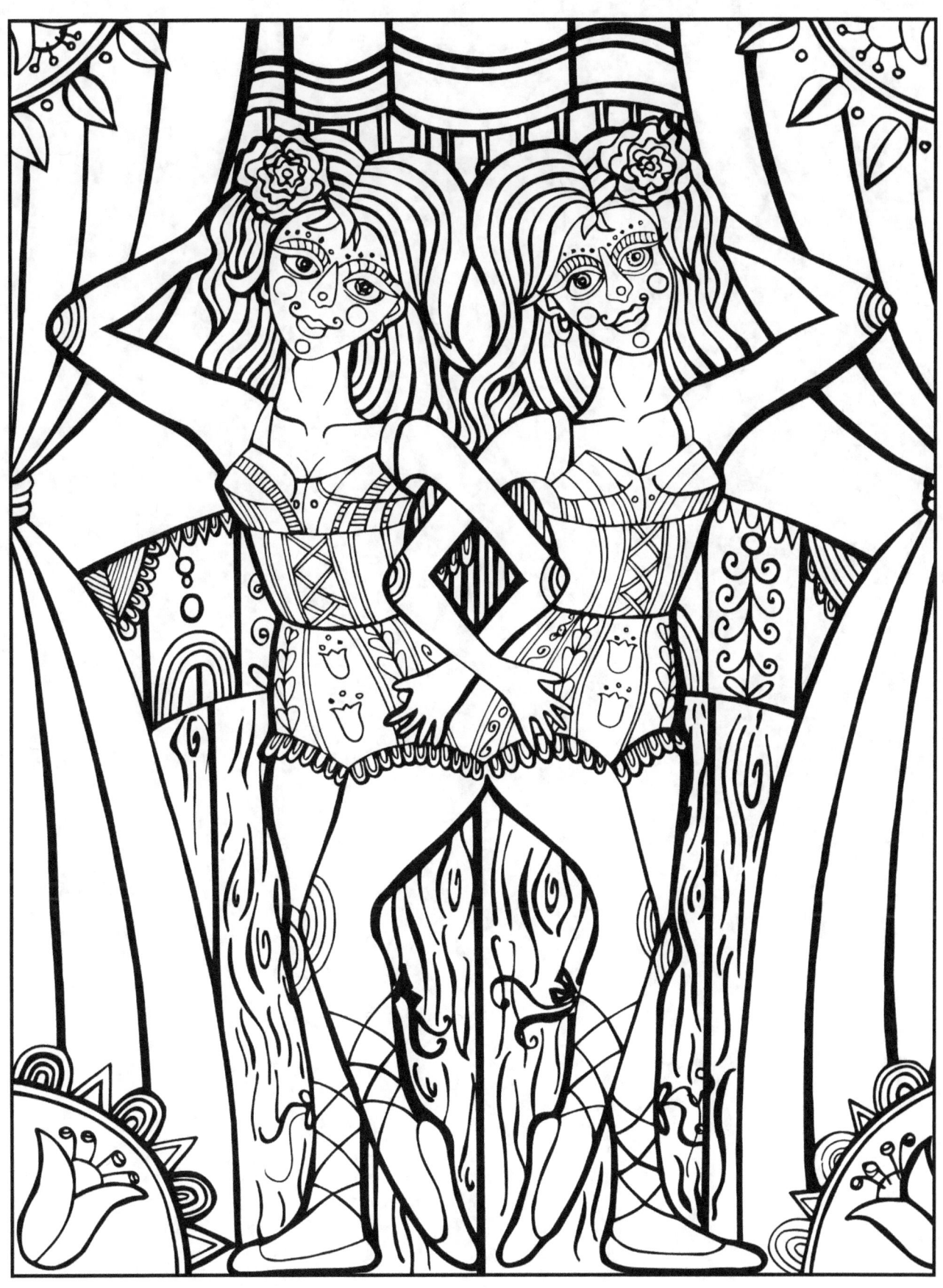

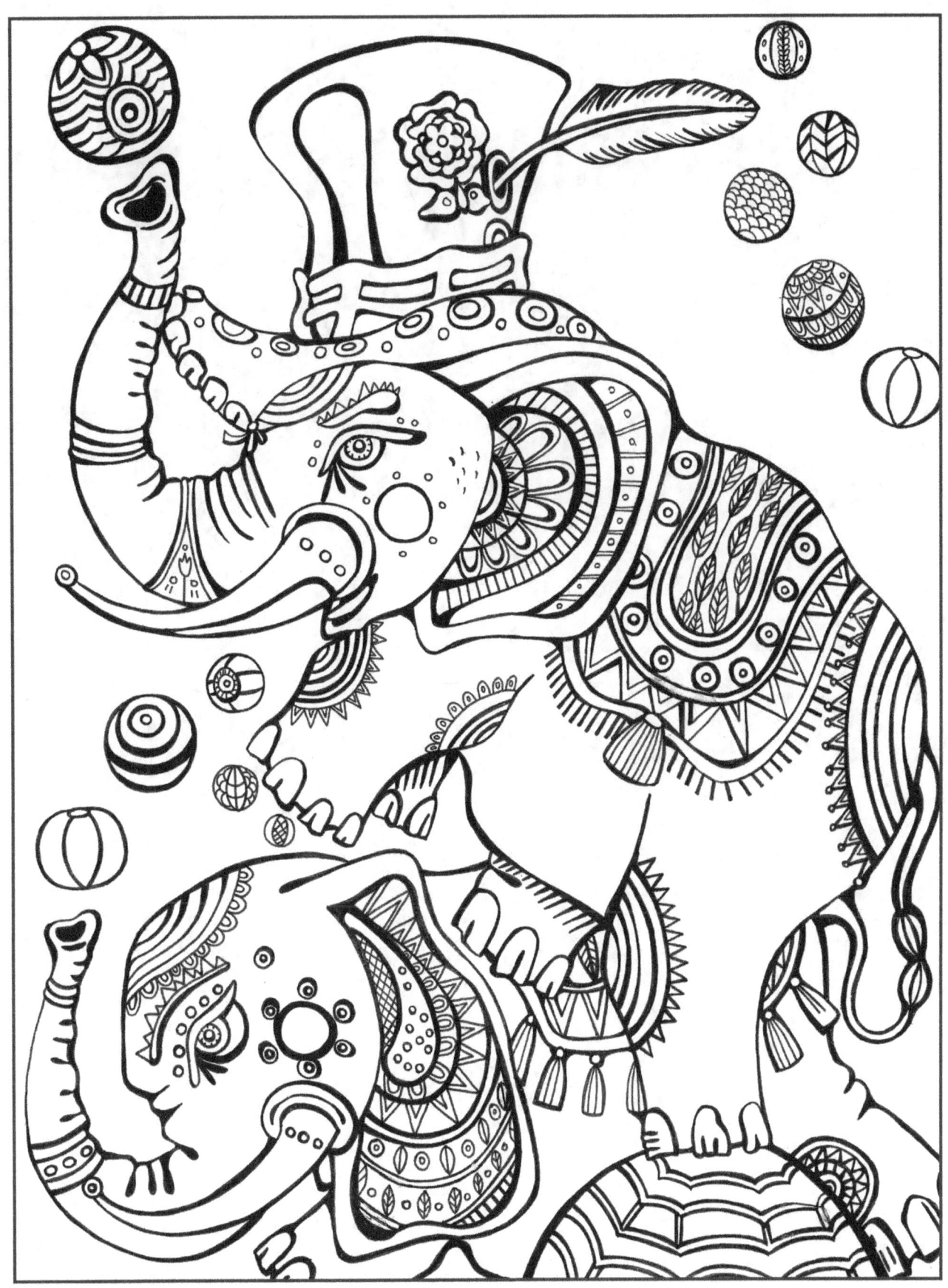

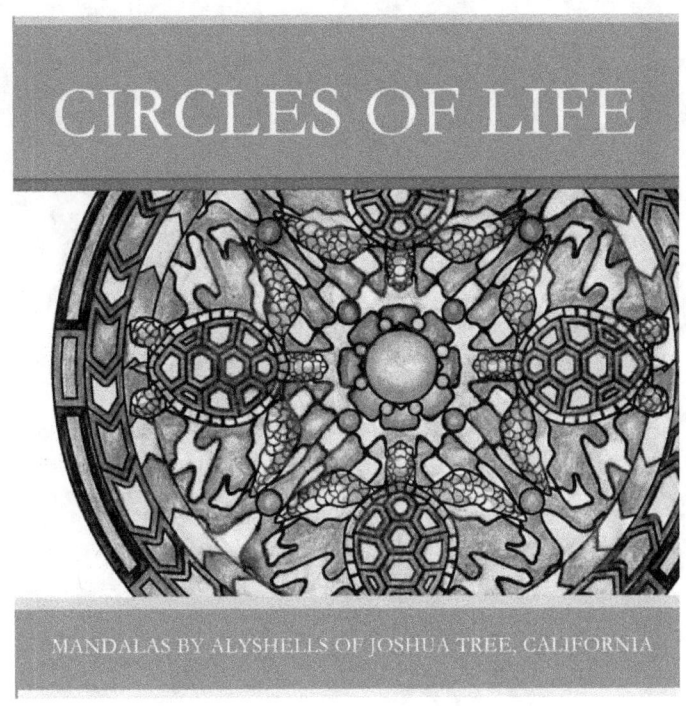

CIRCLES OF LIFE

MANDALAS BY ALYSHELLS OF JOSHUA TREE, CALIFORNIA

This book contains 25 original illustrations created by Alyshells, an artist living in the desert in Joshua Tree, California. Living in the desert has given her a great affinity for the myriad forms of life found on land, in the air and in the sea. Every illustration was conceived with the purpose of showing the awesome variety and beauty of Nature's creations.

An attempt has been made to arrange the illustrations with a progression of difficulty with the easiest early in the book followed by those that are slightly more intricate and challenging. Each provides abundant opportunity for creative expression.

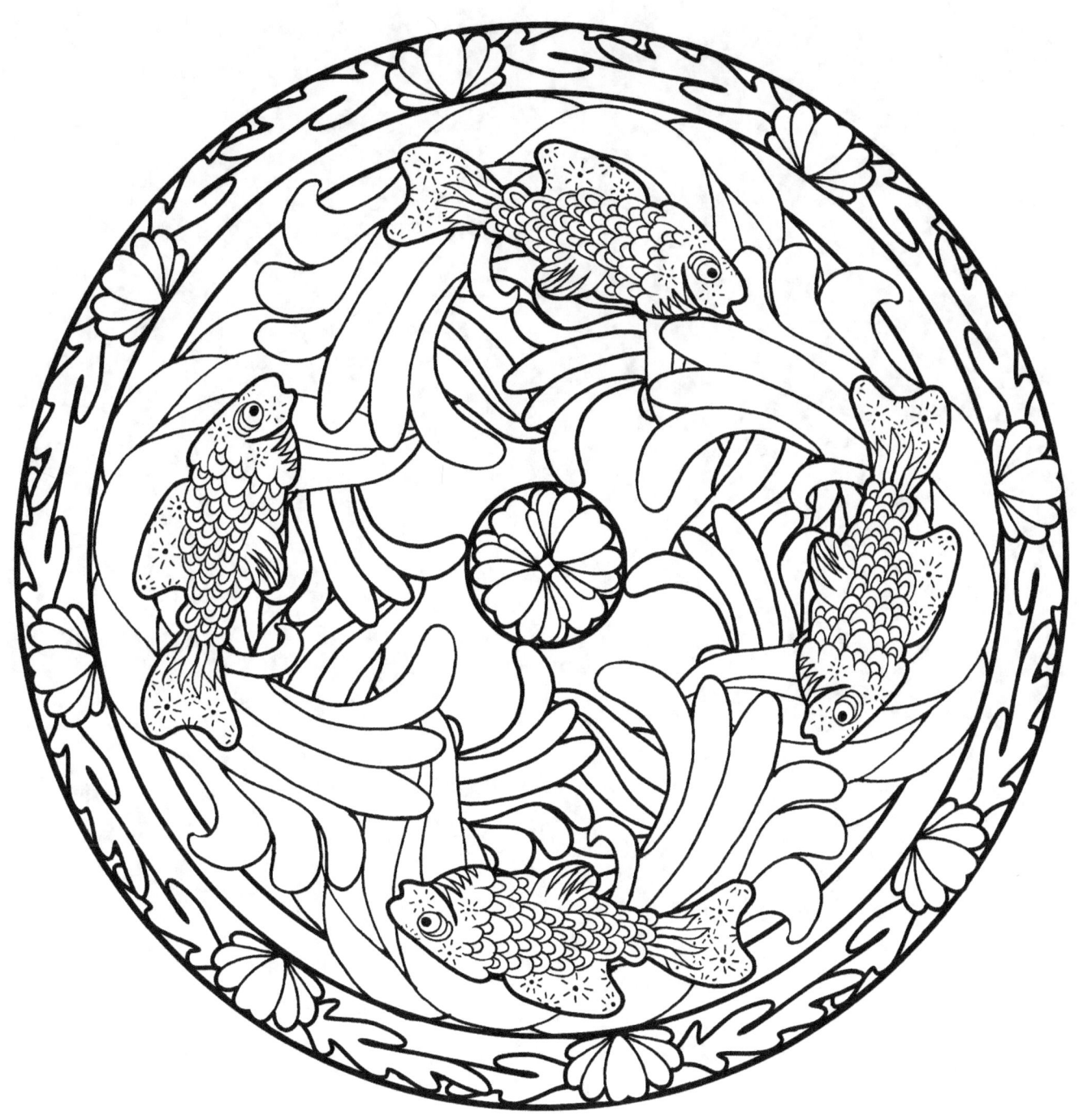

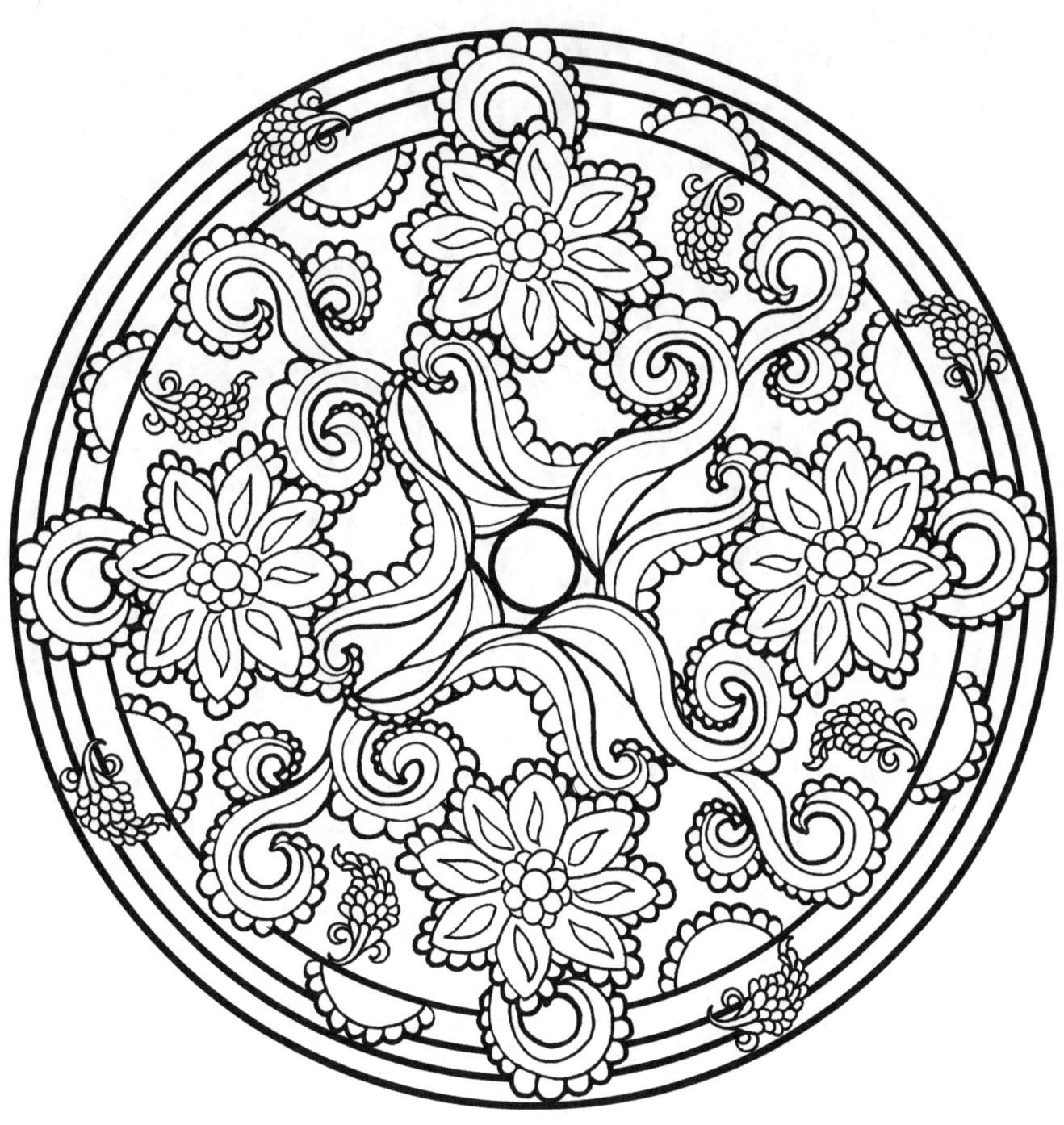

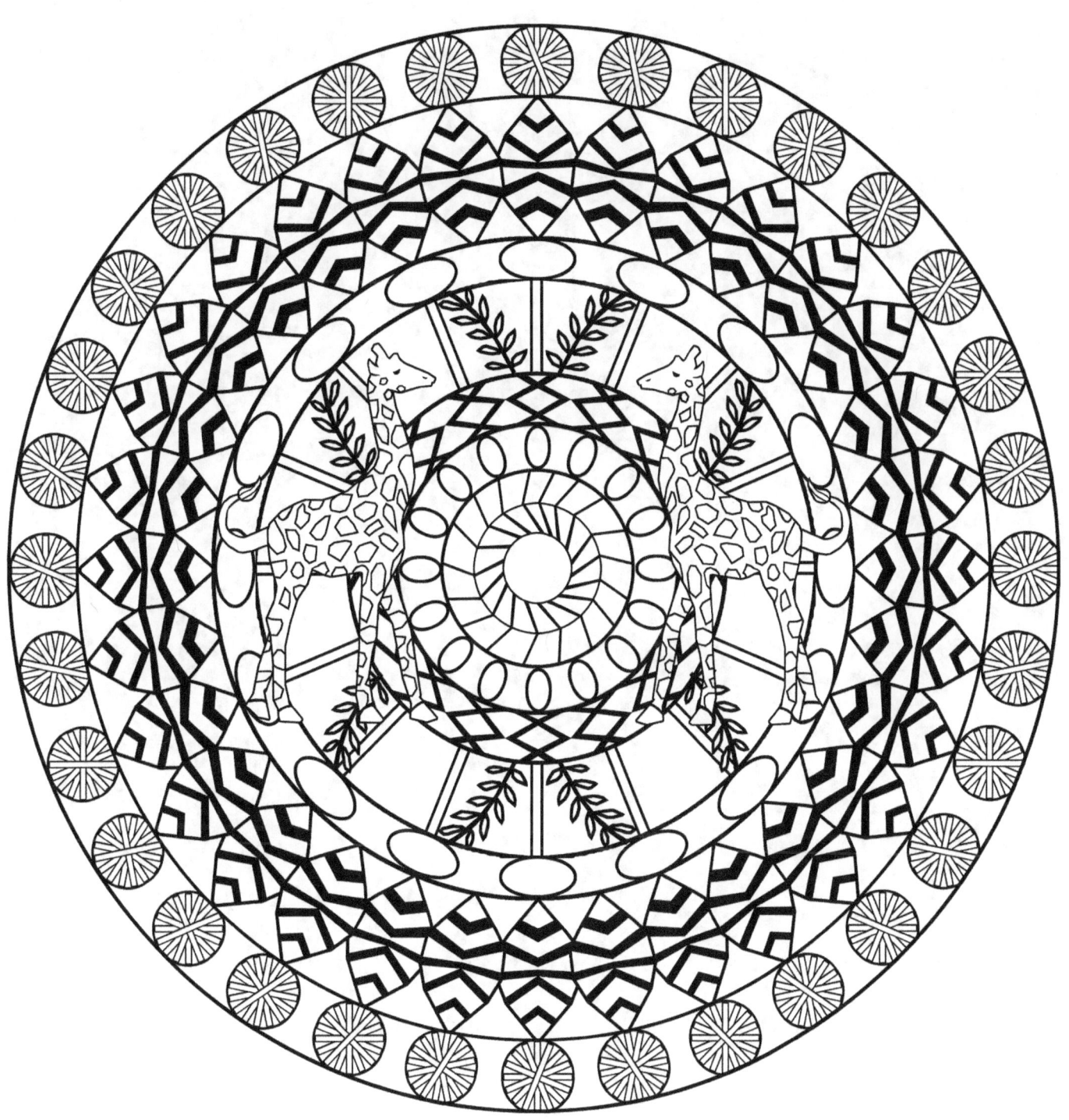

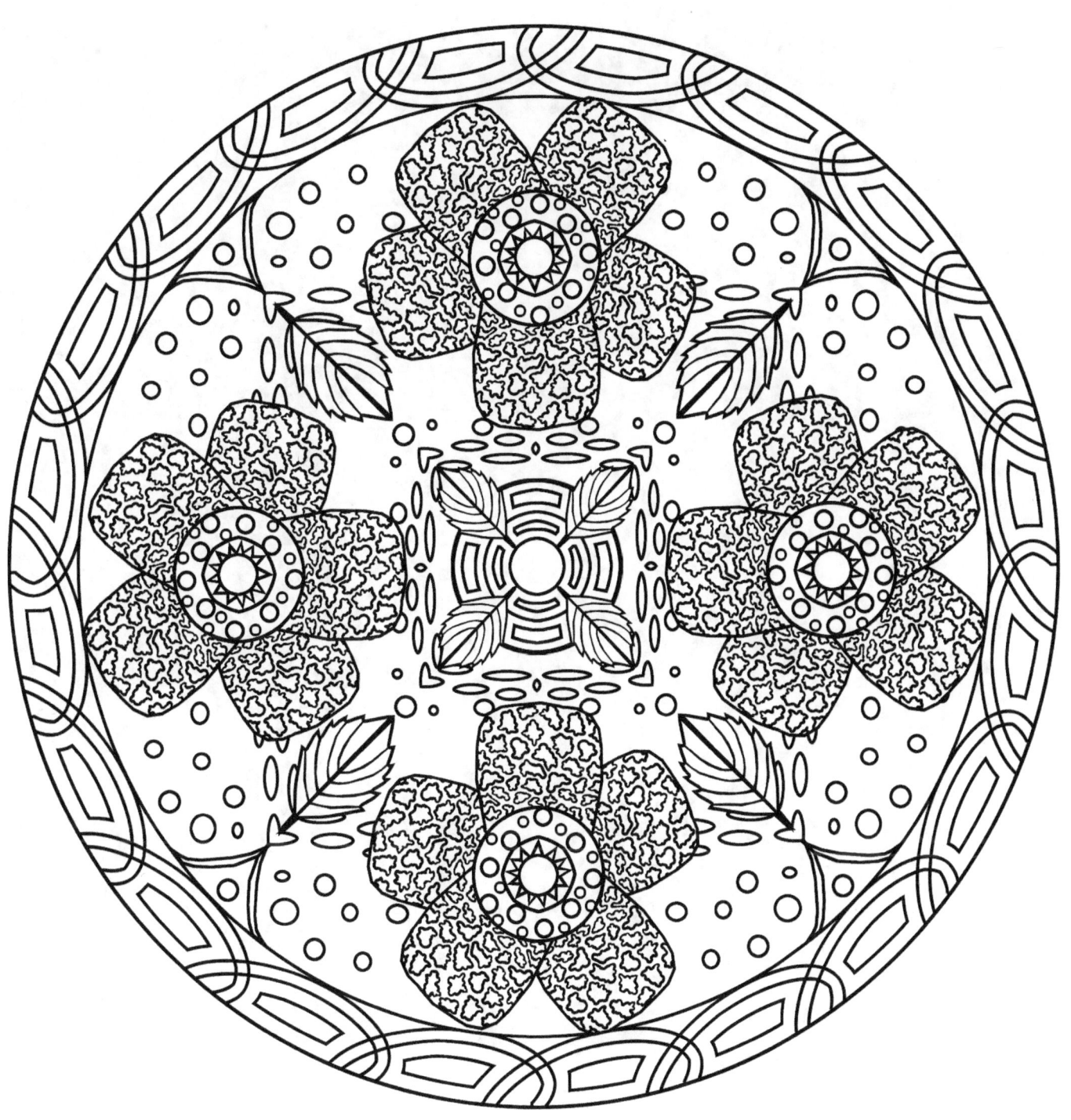

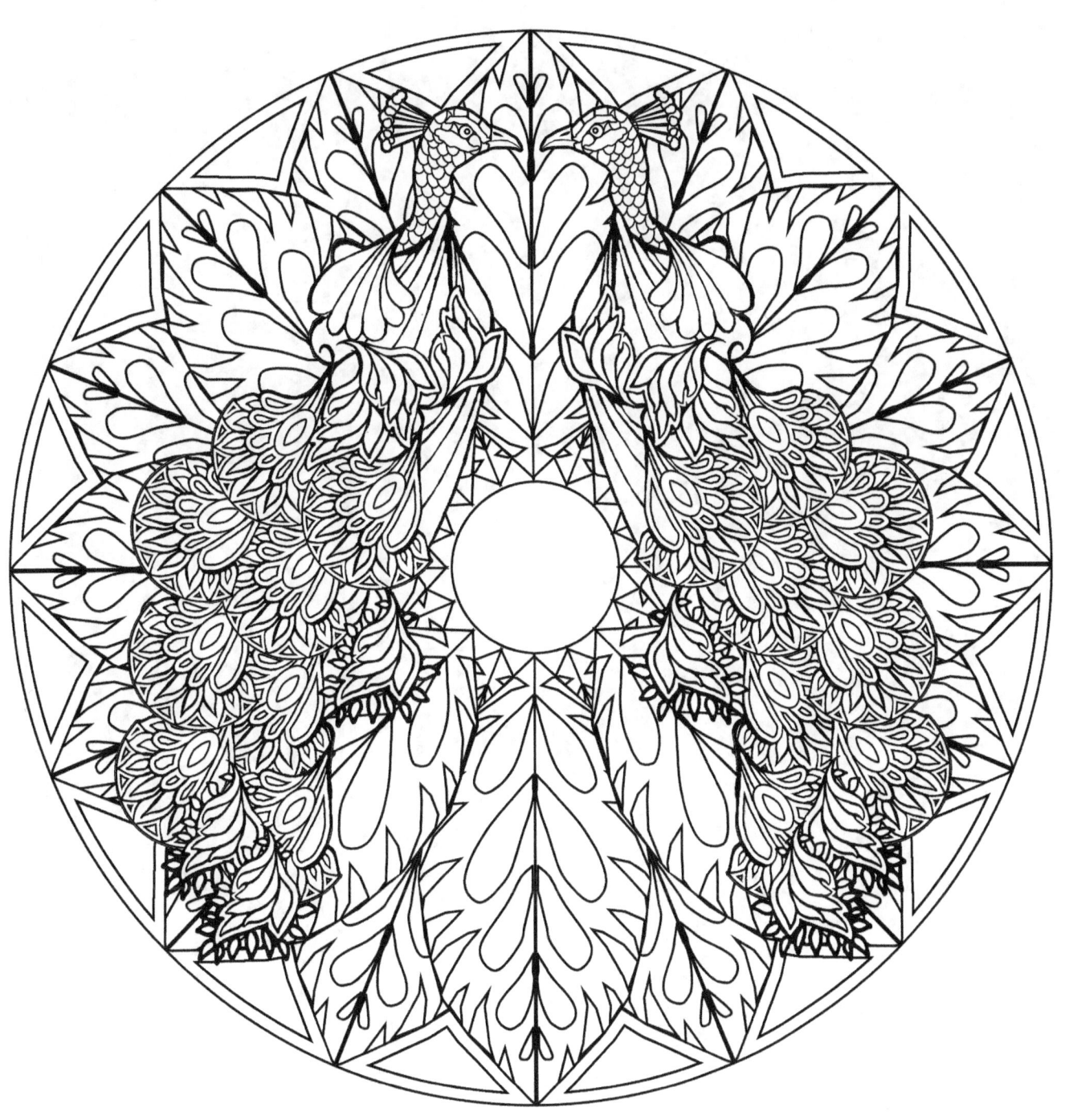

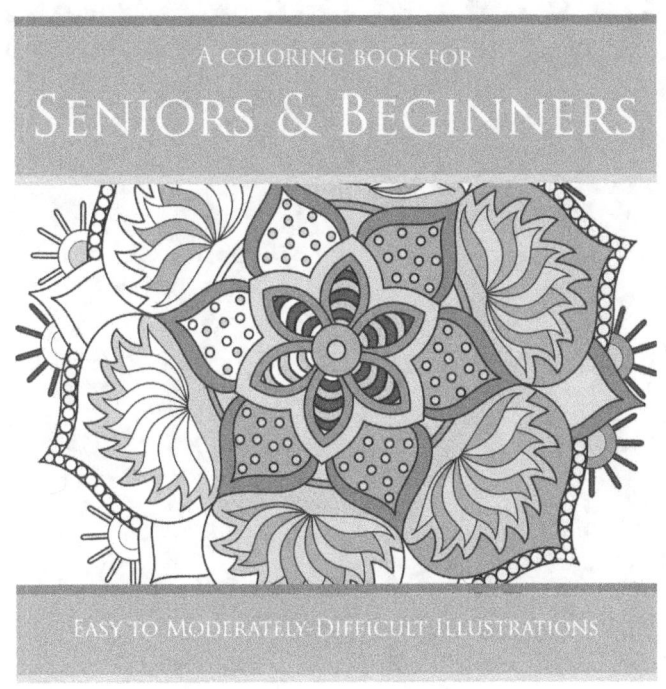

This is a coloring book made especially for people who are not expert colorists or for anyone wanting a simplified and relaxing coloring experience. The benefits of coloring should be available to people at all skill levels. Excessive complexity and microscopic spaces make many best-selling adult coloring books unsuitable for the vast majority of seniors and beginners. Coloring should not be intimidating.

Beginners of all ages may want to gradually undertake the more challenging illustrations. The illustrations in this book will allow them to slowly develop their skills, to develop their confidence, and to experiment with various coloring tools and techniques. The book includes 25 easy to moderately-difficult illustrations.

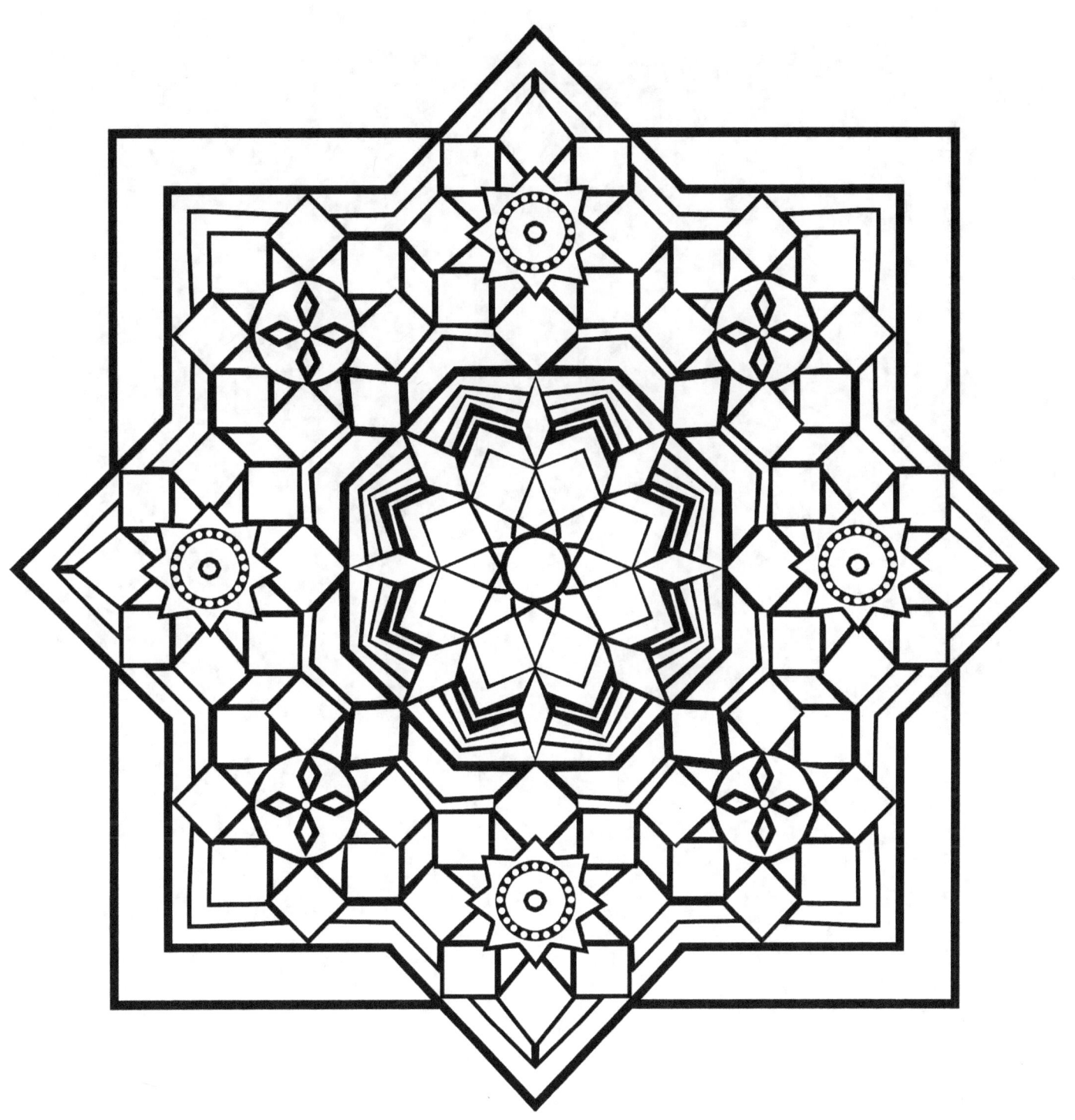

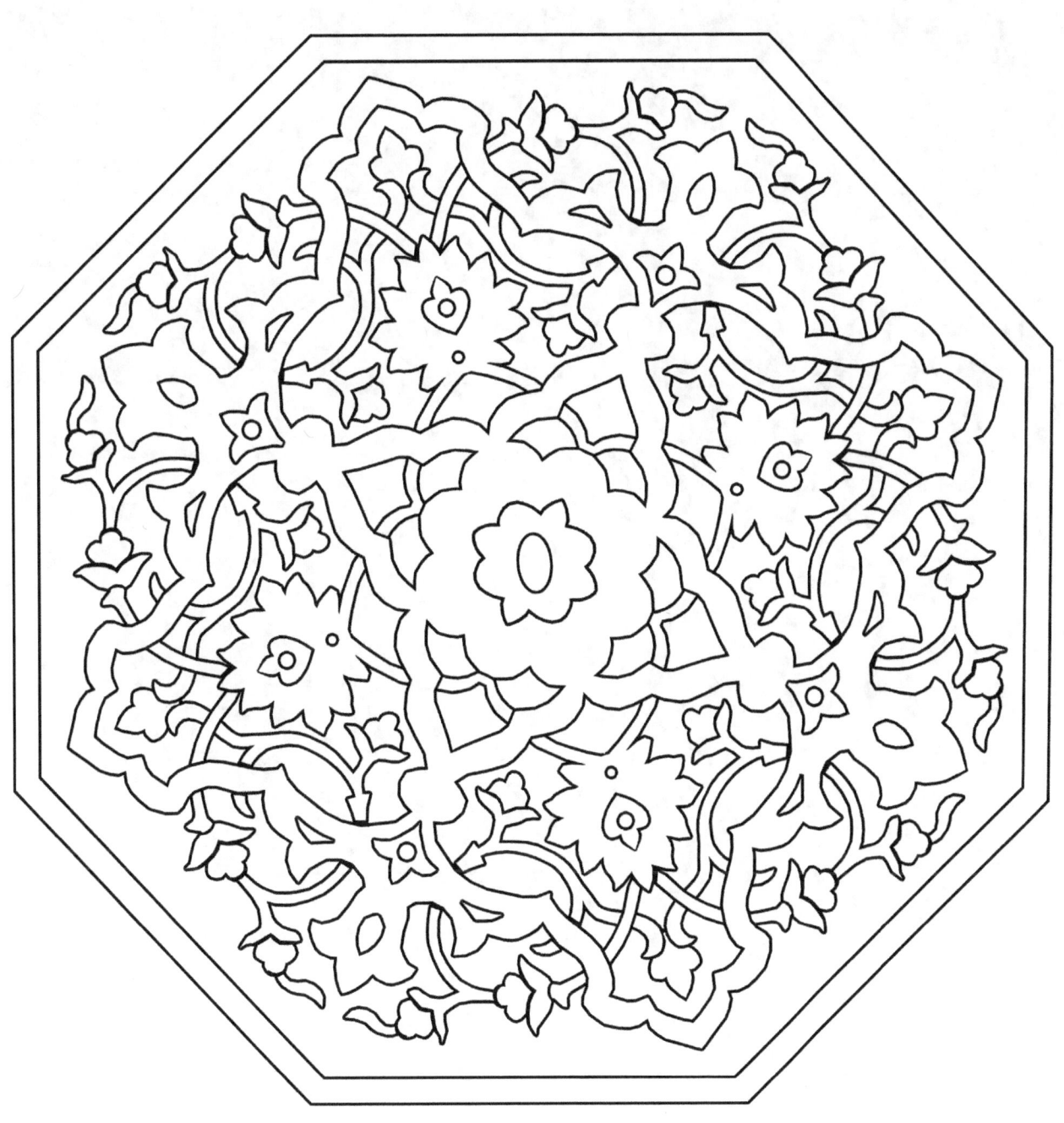

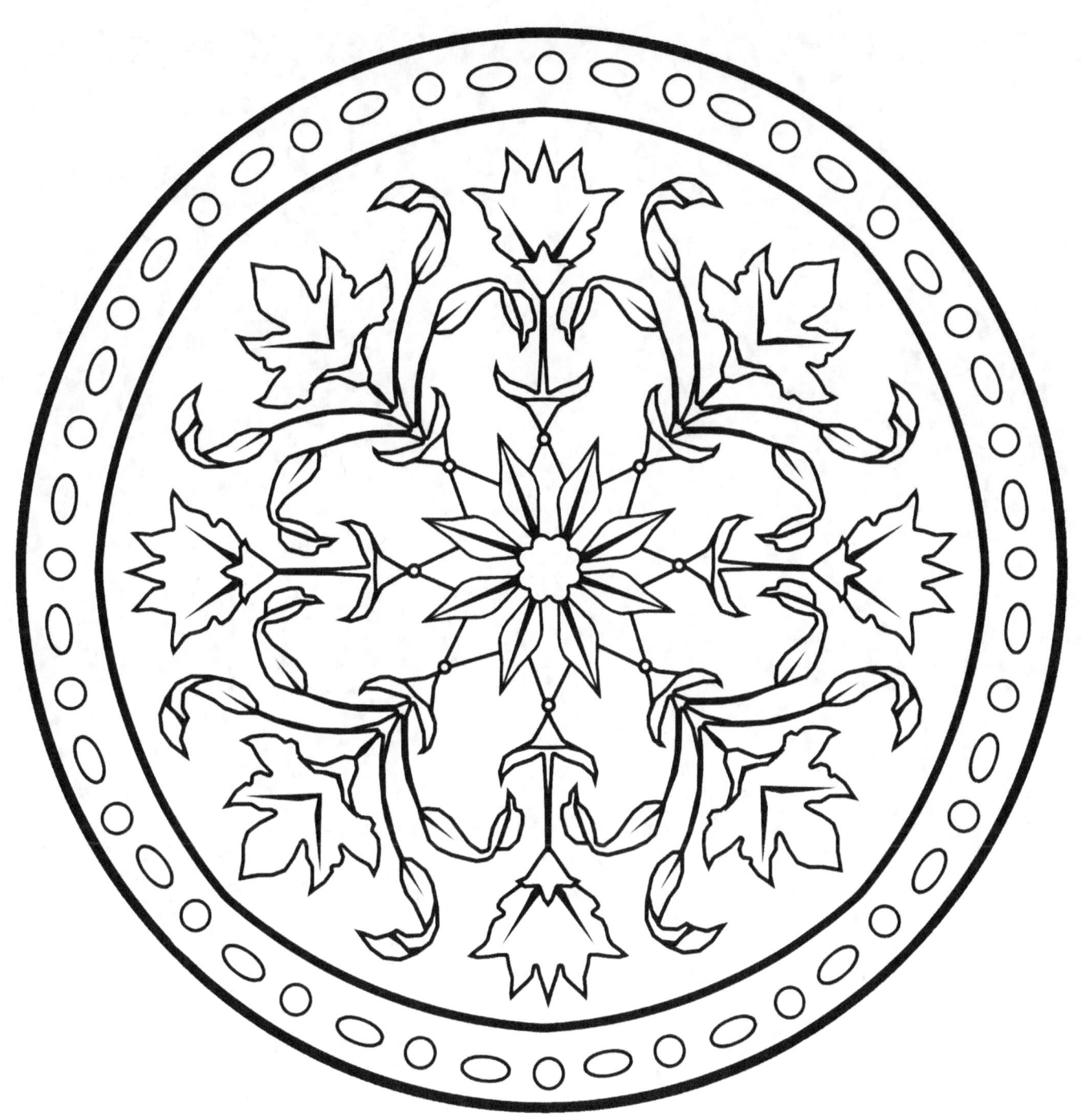

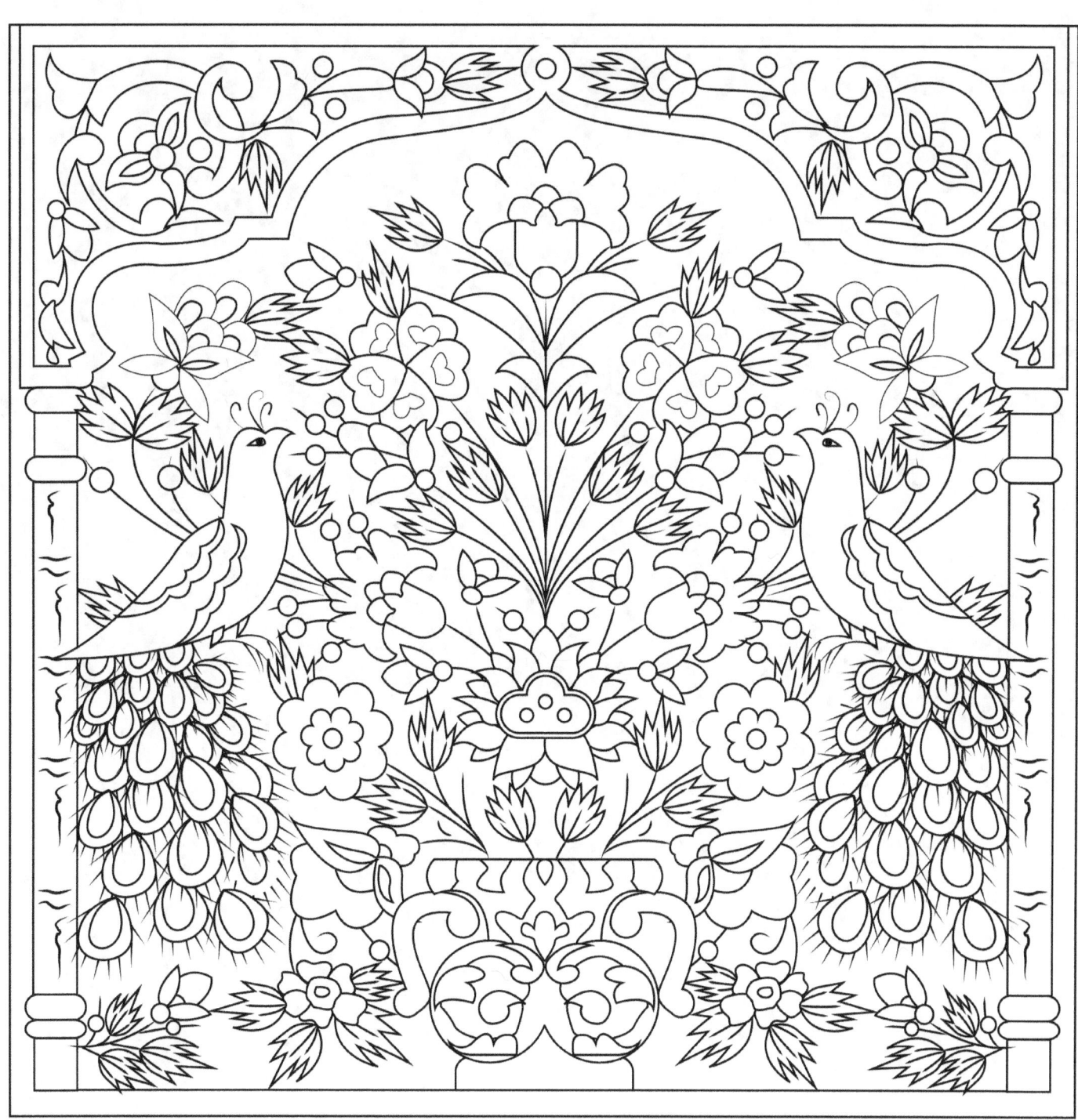

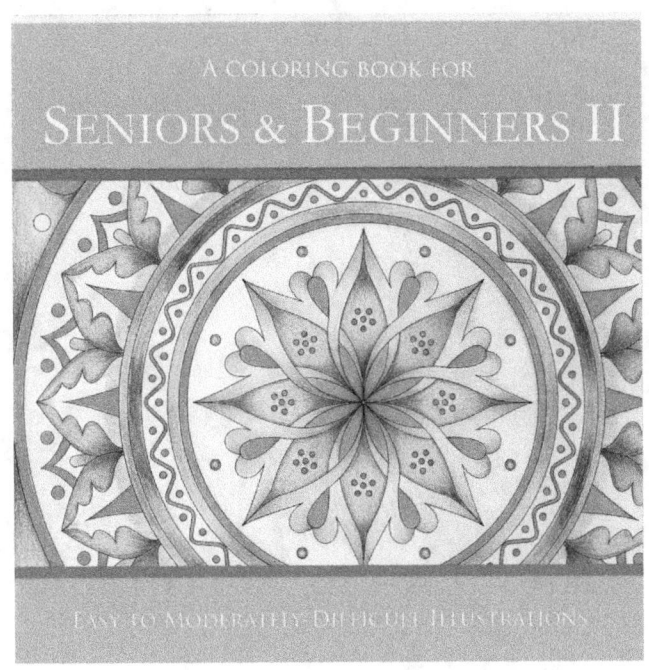

This book is a sequel to our very popular book "Seniors & Beginners," which was published in December 2015. The need for an elementary coloring book became apparent from comments posted by colorists on Facebook and various other forums. Our research tells us that beginners want illustrations that allow them to gradually develop their coloring skills without the anxiety created by overly challenging illustrations, and that seniors want illustrations ideally suited to their levels of dexterity. And, both beginners and seniors want to express their artistic creativity and enjoy all of the psychological benefits of coloring without feeling challenged by the overly-intricate illustrations found in many popular adult coloring books.

This book has an eclectic mix of illustrations that range in difficulty from easy to moderately-difficult. It is our hope that this variety of illustrations will provide you with many hours of coloring pleasure.

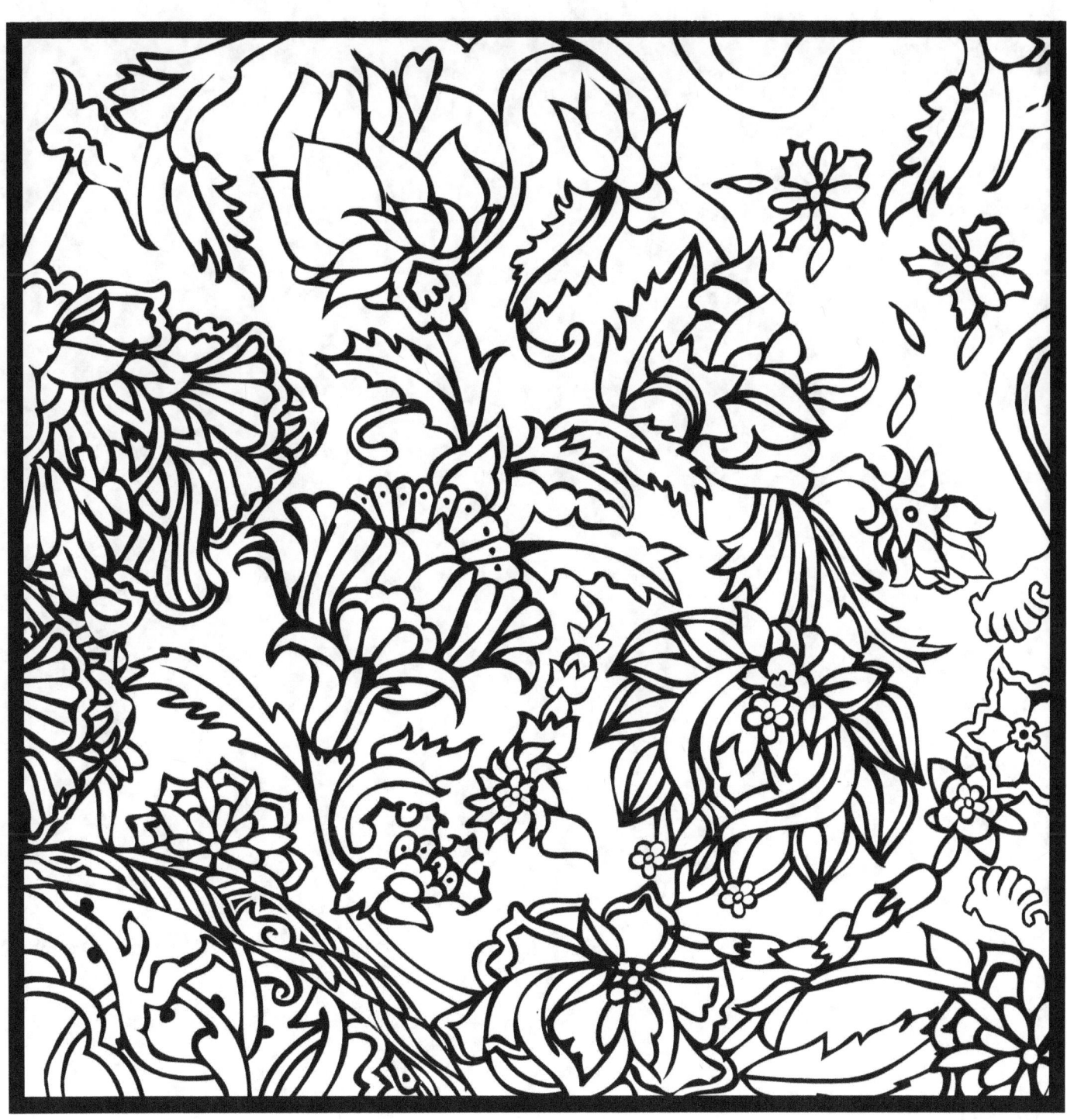

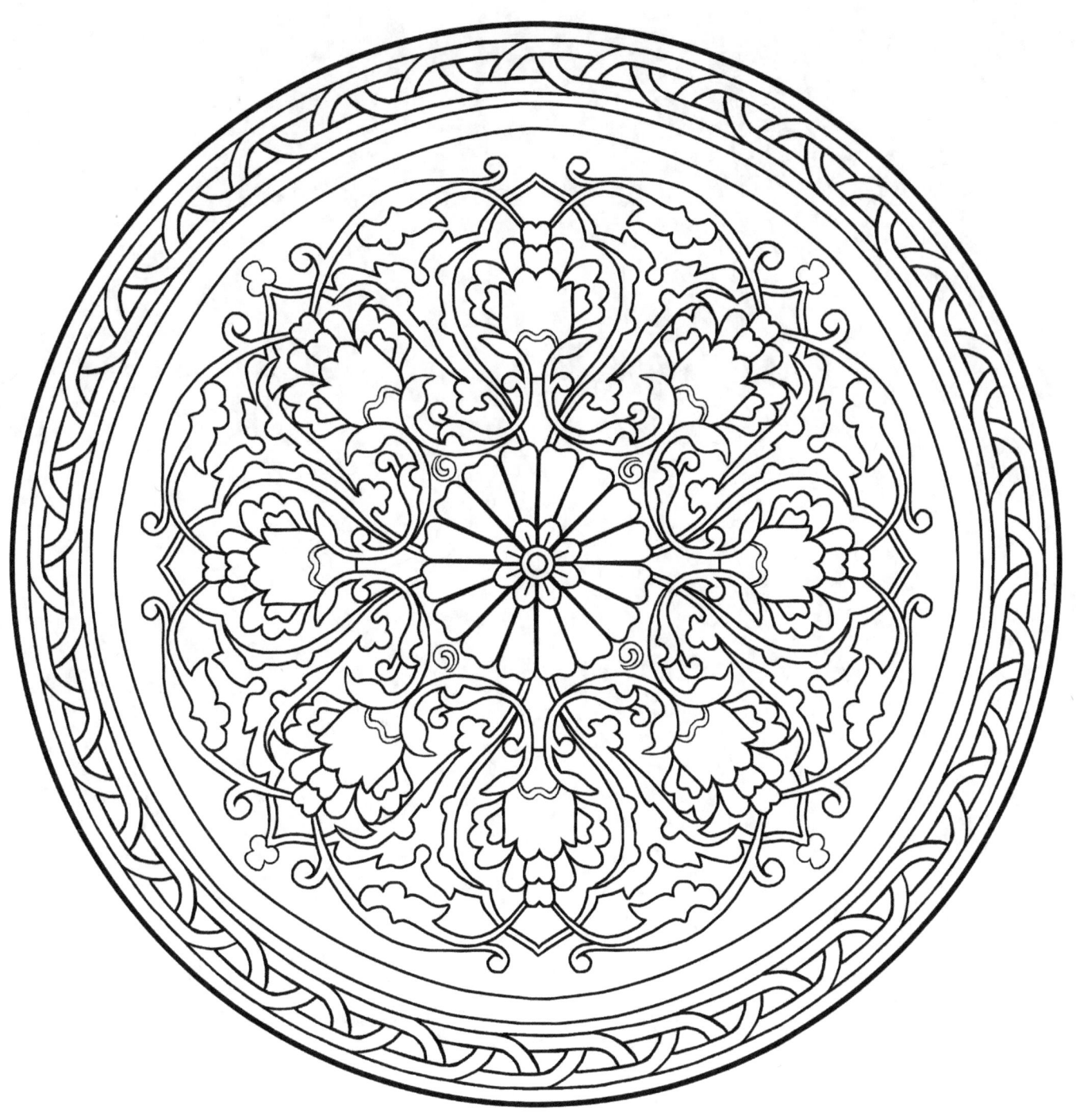

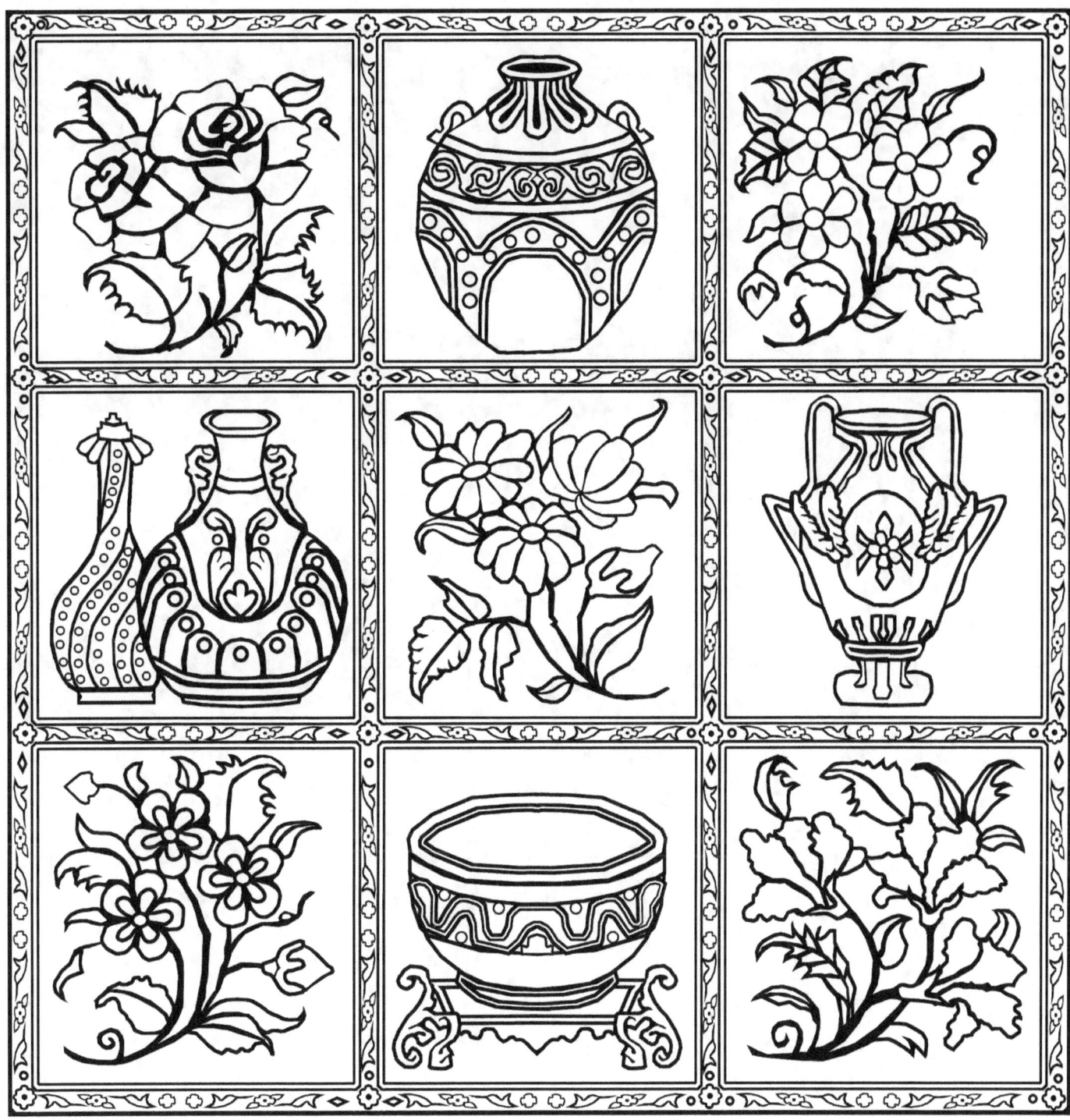

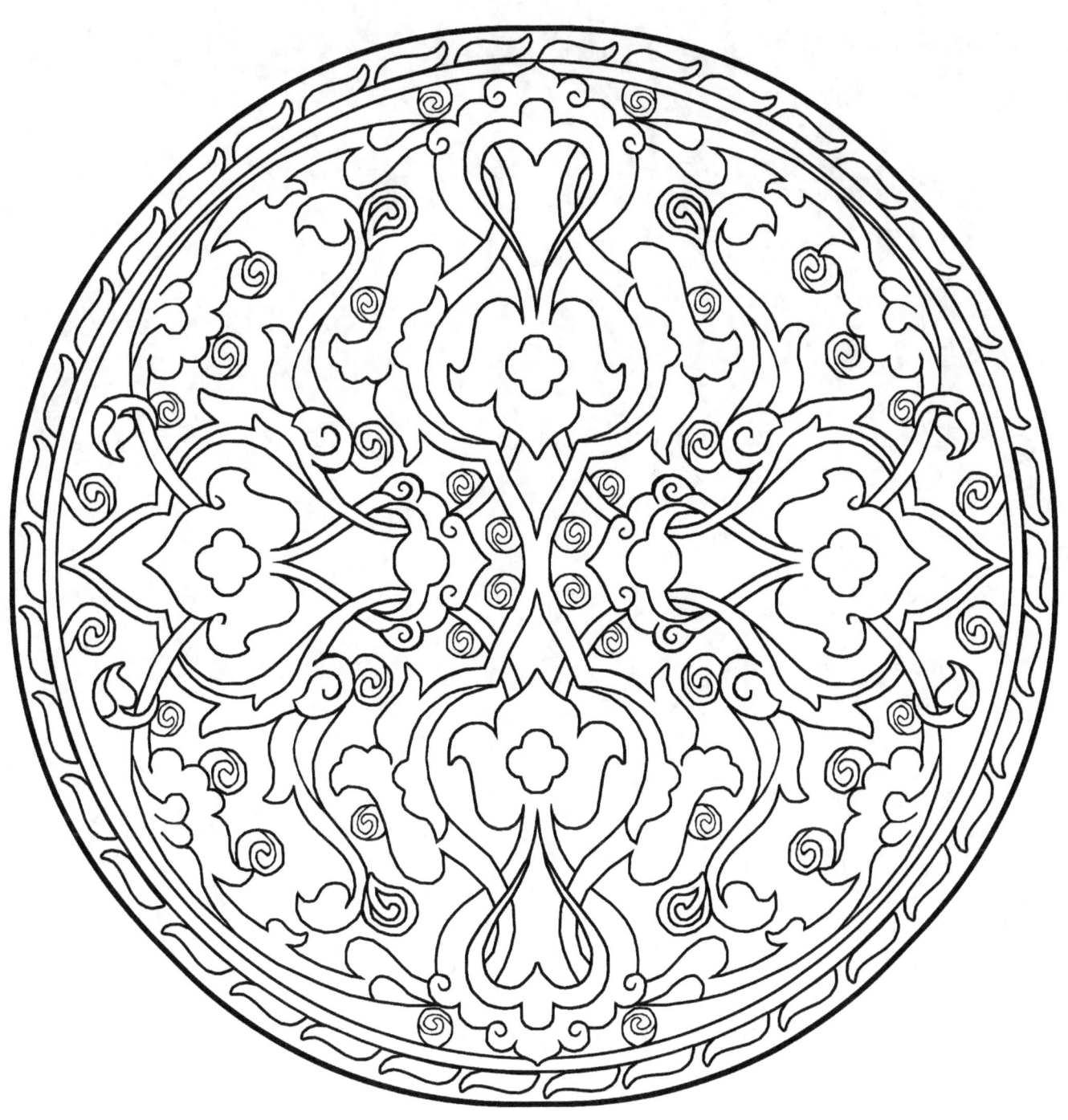